National

Expectations

By

Douglas O'Banion

National Expectations

All Rights Reserved

Copyright © 2025 Anna Justine O'Banion

Table of Contents

Introduction	5
1	
Law and Mercy	9
Part 1 – A Native's Confession	9
Part 2 – A River Named National Security	18
Part 3 – Collectivism, the Cold War, and the Woke Movement	20
Part 4 – A Classical Education	51
Part 5 – Law and Mercy	55
2	
The Rugged Road of Freedom (an old poem)	57
3	
The Parable of the Literalist	61
4	
An Explanation of the Welsh 'Sin-Eater'	67
5	
Practical History	73
6	
Absolute History	77
7	
A Human Condition	81
8	
The Unfairness Confusion	87

9 Romance	91
10 The One and Only Certainty	97
11 The Gift	119
12 Identity	121
13 A Certain Opinion	125
14 Words, Progress, and People	143
15 1985: A Useful Response to George Orwell's novel 1984	153
16 National Treasure	159
17 The Future	163
18 The Great Negotiation	165
19 National Fidelity (a poem)	169
20 My British Ancestor's Eyes	173
21 Natural Law	179
22	

The Crown's Court Opinion (AD 432) 185
23
The Defunct Crown's Court Opinion (AD 2025) 193
Appendix A – 197
A Declaration of Interdependence 197
Reader's Notes 202

Introduction

National Expectations' storyline is fictional. The complete book is classified as epic poetry by its principal author who sees this finished book as evidence that there is more to life than politics, more to justice than popular opinions, more to culture than stereotypes, and more to Western history than names, dates, and blame.

Written in common language in story form, poetry and essays treated with care toward young adult readers and others who may not be familiar with the West, the author of National Expectations examines crucial topics with the aid of ancient oral history and modern Western concerns. While doing so this mostly-British book rests in the middle of the timeless battle between superstition and rationalism: the rugged intellectual soil in which the romantic roots of classical liberalism sprang.

By the use of fictional storytelling, this book leaps through time periods to offer readers fresh insights into traditional topics and current issues, yet the book never strays far from the ever-present British insight that allows the Britons to know that when they cannot out argue their foes, they will outlast them. Rugged Americans share that same ever-present insight.

Americans, British people, and others in most modern Western nations are expected to drop old baggage and to be friendly to our nation's friends, allies to our nation's allies, and to do what we can within reason toward the health of those international relationships. This mostly-British book is in line with those expectations, therefore, even though the book's storyline is fictitious, the book is a serious book, and the book's title *National Expectations; One American's Book for One of America's Allies,* is an honest title.

National Expectations

For
Annie

National Expectations

ISBN: 978-1-62249-755-3
Published by
Biblio Publishing
Columbus, Ohio
BiblioPublishing.com

1
Law and Mercy

Woe to the author who thinks that their written work is more than something worthy of the reader's interpretations.

Similar warnings can be given to aspiring conversationalists.

Part 1 – A Native's Confession

Because historical propaganda is still being printed in history books, today's British people who have heard anything about Native British Queen Boudicca, believe that Rome's politically astute negotiators raped Boudicca's two young daughters, flogged Boudicca only half to death, and that just a few months later my ancestor

National Expectations

Boudicca was somehow healthy enough to physically lead a large army of native Britons to Londinium, where they frightened most of the Romans out of the city before she and other native Britons sacked it.

There is a very low probability that history actually occurred that way, firstly because Boudicca was not a superhero endowed with magical powers of healing that allowed her to recuperate so quickly from emotional and physical damage. Additionally it is very unlikely that The Republic of Rome (The Roman Empire) would spread stories about their raping two young girls unless those stories covered up information that Rome didn't want people to know. For instance, information about King Prasutagus' and Boudicca's two sons, and information about Rome's negotiators in eastern Britain murdering the widowed Queen Boudicca during a standard Roman torture session that left two orphaned British brothers.

If the Roman public had been aware of that information, then the pan-theological mindset of

National Expectations

the superstitious Romans would have caused the Romans to freak themselves out because Rome was supposedly founded by two orphaned brothers (Romulus and Remus). If the Roman public knew that their tortures of native Britons had resulted in two British brothers becoming orphans, the superstitious Roman public would have mistakenly seen the little British brothers as a pan-theological sign of Rome's' impending doom. Or perhaps more accurately written as, Rome's Impending Doom!

Obviously, the Roman Empire didn't need that problematic superstitious news hitting the first-century streets of Rome.

Less obvious is the fact that my native British ancestors didn't want superstitious news spread either, because it likely would have made us look as though we were taking advantage of ignorant people's superstitious signs (people's self-deceptions). That's why we had reason to cover up the problematic facts, just as Rome had reasons to cover up the problematic facts.

National Expectations

Contrary to modern historians' assumptions, my family (King Prasutagus' and Boudicca's family) in eastern Britain was not pagan. We were naturalists, historians, and honest pragmatists who lived by a moral code that was 'Do no harm, unless you must do harm in self defence'.

Therefore, although the coincidence of the orphaned British brothers might have aided us to push Rome off the island of Great Britain, it would have set a horribly inaccurate example for our children as to how we native Britons fought off invaders. We didn't fight hostile invaders off with coincidences and signs. Instead, we used rational conversations first, and if that didn't work, then we confronted them head on and did our best to drive them off our island. Like I said, my first-century British family was not pagan; instead, we were pragmatists (practical people).

In intellectual behaviour, the pagans of long ago (such as first-century Romans) were not much different from modern-day conspiracy theorists who connect whatever dots are available, draw false conclusions, and then enjoy the false comfort

National Expectations

of thinking that they (and perhaps they alone) know what's really going on.

Now I'm going to appear to be a conspiracy theorist to some readers over the next several paragraphs, because I'm going to explain to you the information my ancestors (and other native people) were forced to hide from Rome by placing that information into a few of the famous fables from the British archipelago.

By writing this information I'm going to appear to be a conspiracy theorist because it will appear as if I've connected random dots of information. However, I assure you that neither I nor my ancestors were conspiracy theorists. Instead, we were national security conspirators who were conspiring to stay alive while murderous superstitious Romans occupied our island home.

Because Old Romans, and many other people, in the first century were extremely superstitious and unreasonable, my British ancestors' very old life-saving national security conspiracy was flexibly scheduled to end whenever the public's

National Expectations

superstitions had decreased, and their reasonableness had increased enough that the British public wouldn't make too much or too little out of this oral history I'm sharing with you.

On this issue of people being reasonable, I'd like you to know that the only 'Arthurian' legend attached to my paternal bloodline isn't a story about a king saving Britain so much as it's a story about how Britain is saved by our people's ability to be reasonable with one another.

The full story of how King Prasutagus' and Queen Boudicca's sons were moved to Ireland is a story that contains a lot of interesting bits of information. I'll skip most of those interesting bits so that the most relevant ones stand out to you.

One of those relevant bits of information concerns the national security manoeuvre made when we cut off communications with our British homeland after becoming war refugees in Ireland during the late first century AD.

We had to cut off direct communications because there were too many Roman spies around. Nonetheless, we had to inform our people at home that we had cut off communications. The only way for us to send that message safely was through popular fables that could be told openly and often across both islands.

The particular fable about cutting off communications was the famous story of two giants.

One of those giants was named Fionn MacCumhaill (Finn McCool) while the other giant was named Benandonner. That fable describes Giant's Causeway being toppled into the waters of the North Channel between Scotland and Ireland. That fable also hinted at children hiding in order to avoid a physical confrontation. Additionally, in its original form that fable made one reference to intellect being used as a weapon rather than merely as a defence.

After that fable reached our lands in Britain, the native Britons in Wales answered with a story about two large dragons, a wizard, a king, and a young boy. The entire story eventually became the much shorter version that today offers only a fraction of the metaphors and information that the original story did. Today's short version tells a story of how the national flag of Wales came to feature a red dragon.

I was told that after arriving in Ireland during the first century AD, the Irish gave my ancestor and his brother a covert Gaelic-sounding name that was a reference to my ancestor Queen Boudicca. That covert name was Ui Bhanain.

I can't speak or read the Irish language. But by way of dictionaries, I know that Ui translates into English as the words 'from', 'son of', or 'grandson of'. I also know that the Irish word bhan is associated with the words 'bean', 'woman', and 'lady'. Therefore, I can only guess that the ain suffix stems from the Irish number one a haon (pronounced 'ah hain'). With those things accounted for I estimate that in Irish Gaelic my British ancestor's covert name Ui Bhanain meant 'From the First Lady'.

National Expectations

After receiving that covert name in Ulster, where the stories of Finn McCool began, my native British ancestor and his brother were escorted by the O'Carroll clan southwards into central Ireland, where they camped at a spot of land that today is the tiny village named Coolderry.

Coolderry is like our home town of Thetford, England, in as much as both are located near county lines. Coolderry was made more like Thetford when the O'Carroll clan's chief became the Earl of Ely O'Carroll. That allowed my family to live near a place named Ely in Ireland like we would have had we lived at home in Thetford.

As for the English translation of the O'Banion name, the ban-ion portion of my name literally means in Irish Gaelic 'white-pure'. That's not a reference to the white race. Instead, it's a reference to my paternal line's obligation to someday 'come clean' (confess) publicly about this old history. I have confessed it here. Now it's time to move on.

Part 2 – A River Named National Security

For younger readers' sake I've tried to avoid needlessly complicating this book's national security theme. The only way to avoid needless complexity is to keep things simple. Therefore, I'd like you to consider this entire book as a river that has formed from several smaller tributary streams.

One of those tributaries is called National Resiliency. It pertains to the national security I described in part 1 of this chapter.

Another tributary in this river analogy is a tributary called Trust.

Another tributary is called Classical Education.

Another tributary is what former Prime Minister David Cameron called 'The Big Society'. The basics of this 'Big Society' idea can be summed up in one word: volunteerism.

It's extremely dangerous for everyone's every need to be placed in the lap of government. That's dangerous because if a domino falls (and they do occasionally fall), that one domino can negatively affect the whole of the government and everyone's every need under a Big Government nanny state.

Big Governments can fall very hard, and when they do they can damage a lot of people.

Inversely, Big Societies such as former Prime Minister David Cameron outlined during his tenure don't fall so dramatically because they're local, responsive, less-bureaucratic, flexible, forgiving, forgivable, and they produce by-products that enrich people's lives.

Those by-products are personal relationships, dignity, fulfilment, genuine compassion, honesty, authenticity, and similarly good things that can altogether be described with a capital 'h', Humanity.

'Big Societies' are sustainable through easy times and hard times. 'Big Governments' are not.

The last tributary I'll mention regarding this analogous river is a tributary called Counter-Extremism. That topic is addressed in part 3 of this chapter.

Part 3 – Collectivism, the Cold War, and the Woke Movement

Sometimes the easiest way to understand an ideology is to understand how it evolved over time. I'll begin explaining the Woke crowd's ideological evolution from the starting point of 21 February 1848. That was the date that Karl Marx and Friedrich Engels published their infamous book *The Communist Manifesto*.

Decades after that extremist book became popular in Eurasia, General Secretary Joseph Stalin was elected in 1922. Then in 1933, Chancellor Adolf Hitler was placed into office by way of backroom negotiations combined with popular elections.

General Secretary Stalin and Chancellor Hitler both built massive bureaucracies in order to govern more and more of their people's individual choices.

After many Westerners saw those two Marxist bureaucracies portrayed in a fashionable glow of capital c 'Change' and 'Industrial Hope', Progressive Westerners who were attached to universities jumped at the opportunity to operate as Marxist salesmen in books and university lecture halls.

Because Marxist ideologies were being taught in Western universities, concerned Westerners were able to study Marxist ideology's academic details. There weren't many.

That study into Marxist ideology ended with no actionable conclusions.

Among the non-actionable conclusions arrived at by concerned Westerners was one suggesting that they (concerned Westerners) had become somewhat paralysed after observing that our Western understanding *He who governs best governs least was* being replaced with its opposite, which is the Marxist understanding *He who governs best governs most.*

Both the Western and the Marxist understandings of that era were extreme. Therefore, it seemed reasonable to Westerners that they should sit back and allow these two extreme ideological concepts balance themselves in some natural way.

Not all countries followed that example of patience or paralysis. Therefore, it came to pass that Marxist ideals were poured out by Hitler and Stalin all over their people during the early part of the mid-twentieth century.

When that occurred, Marxist collective ideology married with a communal morality that sent their people's intellect out to pasture on a wide-open plane of unfulfilled personal duties where a person's individual psychology and spirit were rendered obsolete.

From the socialists' and communists' perspective, that death of the individual person's spirit was justified because they all served *The Collective*. It was mass suicide of the spirit in the hope of equalizing material things.

Human freewill is not a material thing. Therefore, freewill holds little or no value within the ideological framework of most communal societies.

After the early twentieth century's Marxist revolutions occurred, both far-left and far-right Marxist countries' people found that their personal freedom and individual psychology were of no practical use. Their minds were free only to dream dreams that seemed to be non-actionable because the State controlled everyone and virtually everything.

The emotional result of those things was that people felt a sense of emptiness that could be medicated by either that person running away from those countries or surrendering to it all while reading books that told readers that their emptiness was universally unavoidable, and that a sense of one's own emptiness was the natural way for any intelligent person to feel.

People found that sort of book when they rediscovered a dead mad man's writings.

That dead mad man's name was Friedrich Nietzsche. People in Marxist countries and some

National Expectations

Western countries fondly read Nietzsche's philosophy, which is most often referred to as nihilism.

Nihilism offered empty people of any nation a compelling argument for why they should give up on life, accept the fact that they really aren't worth anything, and accept soulless emptiness as being natural for all intelligent people to feel.

Even today in the early twenty-first century, people who want to justify their own emptiness, or people who want to pretend that they're more intelligent or more Woke than other people, find Nietzsche's nihilistic writing to be a comfort.

Such books sold a lot of emptiness around the world. No Western country's universities went untouched by Nietzsche's emptiness and, later, Jean-Paul Sartre's books that sold absurdity and nothingness.

I suspect that Friedrich Nietzsche and Jean-Paul Sartre were suffering from the sort of blindness that comes from a person's astonishingly ambitious belief that they have seen

National Expectations

through everything. C.S. Lewis mentions that sort of blindness at the end of his insightful book *The Abolition of Man*.

The empty ideals in Nietzsche's and Sartre's books, as well as other empty books, did only minor damage to British society on the whole because British society maintained respect for individual people. Nonetheless, the empty communal ideas of Marxism along with Nietzsche's nihilism and Sartre's philosophy of 'nothingness' did a great deal of damage to people who willingly walked down the dark path towards pop-nihilism as 'Salvation through Scepticism'.

That sort of pop-nihilism was sold by the ambitious contrarian Christopher Hitchens.

While he sold that, another sort of pop-nihilism was sold in the form of 'Salvation through Science'. It was sold by authors and activists such as the methodically minded myopic materialist Richard Dawkins.

I think that if Hitchens were still alive today he would say that my previous paragraphs had a fatal

National Expectations

flaw in it because there was no salvation that he was selling. However, 'Salvation' was exactly what Mr. Hitchens was selling when he attempted to save his audience from other people's notions of salvation. When one writes a book, or gives a speech, or argues with people in order to pull them away (save them) from something, then that person is presenting a sort of salvation. Hitchens did, and Dawkins still does, offer their audience salvation by way of one sort of materialism or another. The difference between Hitchens and the other sort of materialist is that although they all could easily take your Christmas dinner and replace it with a map of the physical universe, a statistical calculator, and copies of their books, perhaps only Hitchens would tell you that he had his doubts as to whether or not you and your family would ever thank them for it.

I studied various ideological books on these subjects for several years before I felt confident enough in my findings to establish two hypotheses. One was my hypothesis that writers of empty nonsense (authors such as Nietzsche and

Sartre) are inclined towards the blindness that C.S. Lewis mentioned in *The Abolition of Man*. Yet many of the people who bought into those empty books suffered from a different sort of blindness. It's a blindness shared by many materialists and collectivists who either can't, or who choose not to, look inward. *Note: looking inward is called introspection.*

That hypothesis may never be proved. Nonetheless, it can be examined as follows...

Some people are skilled painters because they see things that other people don't see. Natural variation in how individual human beings see the world (intellectual variation) has probably aided human survival and development over hundreds of thousands of years. Therefore, there is a fair chance that intellectual variation has been ingrained into our DNA, and that that variation would occasionally result in the sorts of intellects that sceptics and anti-religious scientists have. It seems to me that those intellects, through no fault of their own, just don't see introspectively.

National Expectations

Not being able to see introspectively is a limitation that causes intellectual myopia which can lead science activists such as (name redacted) to understand that the sciences of biology, psychology, and statistics can easily lead one to predict the existence of some people who are born blind to seeing in an introspective manner. Their scientifically trained minds are willing to admit that those sorts of intellectual anomalies exist, yet they don't want to think themselves to be an anomaly. To them what can be observed by way of introspection doesn't exist.

That sort of intellectual myopia can lead materialists to believe that they can see everything that the world's greatest oil painters can see. And that the only reason that they themselves can't become great oil painters is that their hands lack the dexterity for it. In their view, they're capable of seeing everything that Mary Shelly saw while she wrote her literary masterpiece *Frankenstein*. But that they can't match the high level of Mary Shelly's writing because they lack the vocabulary for it.

But, please don't get me wrong here. I appreciate the hard sciences for multiple reasons. For instance, the lights in my flat are working right now due in part to scientific advancements. Soon I may pull a frozen meal from my freezer and then microwave it so that I can eat a quick lunch before getting back to my work writing this book. Aside from the food that comprises my lunch this afternoon, the other things that keep my food fresh and then allow me to cook it are also natural, because nature (particularly the laws of physics) is required in order for technology, science, and scientific advancements to exist. Nonetheless, most people disregard the source of physics so that they can chisel it all down to the soulless single term 'science'.

Therefore, even though nature produced everything that will go into my lunch this afternoon, materialists will chalk it up to scientific advancements in agriculture, as well as modern manufacturing of freezers and microwave ovens.

But regardless of what words we use to describe these things, I don't like to bite the scientific hand that feeds me, and then sends me an electric bill for it every month. That's just one of the many reasons why I'm not anti-science.

I'm very appreciative of how much medical science and other sciences have improved the quality of life of so many people. Nonetheless, it's worth mentioning that some science extremists are like a deaf person who wants to enjoy their meal in a public restaurant, yet can't enjoy it because they're overly anxious about not understanding why so many of the other diners in the restaurant are tapping their feet every time the restaurant plays a foot-tapping-worthy piece of music over the restaurant's speakers.

'What the hell is going on?' they wonder. Then they might text their deaf friends on their smart phones and find out that their friends are also freaking out and texting them on their smart phones, 'I don't know exactly what is going on with this foot-tapping thing either. But as I understand it, if you tap your feet, then after you die you go to heaven, which is great. And if you don't tap your feet, then after you die you go to hell, where you will burn for eternity.'

With that sort of situation being the case for some people who simply don't understand Christianity, I can understand why they're frustrated. I mean that if the shoe were on the other foot, then I'd be frustrated if Bill Nye the Science Guy told me that I'd burn in hell for eternity if I didn't make a pilgrimage to see Le Grand – K in Saint Cloud, France.

I understand those people's frustration. That's one of the reasons that I've not included comments about the afterlife in this book.

I hope that any anti-religious people who are reading this book appreciate my efforts towards understanding their frustration. I also hope that they return the favour by at least admitting to themselves that Le Grand – K has no freewill, and that neither Le Grand – K or Charles Darwin were conscious when life began.

During the decades of the Cold War Western national security depended heavily on our

National Expectations

winning the technology race against the Marxist East. Therefore, Western leaders accepted the unavoidable deferred cost associated with pushing hard science on to Western societies. The unavoidable deferred cost was paid by their technology-centric children's and grandchildren's generation's turning cold during the Cold War.

Keeping up with the 'global Jones' is still important, and the technological advancements that entails are important too. But the Cold War is over. The current war between Ukraine and Russia highlights the fact that the Cold War (a race between Western and Eastern military technology) is over now. Both sides won that race when large-scale nuclear disarmament took place beginning in 1987 with the INF Treaty (Intermediate-Range Nuclear Forces Treaty), and then continuing with additional treaties such as the START 1 Treaty (Strategic Arms Reduction Treaty) in 1991.

Peaceful relations continue to be worked towards (with some difficulty) by East and West via treaties such as the United States–Russia

Strategic Stability Dialogue (SSD) treaty in 2021. The Cold War is over. Now it's time to get back to the basics, and the balance of a classical education.

I began studying ideology before I knew what the word 'ideology' really meant. For instance when I was ten years old I studied it by analysing my own reactions to Carl Sagan's messages put forth in his PBS television programme *Cosmos*.

While paying close attention to my emotions and that broadcast, I noticed interesting things such as how Carl Sagan used an almost hypnotic catch phrase every time he referred to the number of this or that as being numbered in the 'billions, and billions, and billions'. His tone, posture, hand gestures, and facial expression of wonder mixed with self-satisfaction were all components of an effective messaging of materialism that left young viewers feeling filled up by imagination and grand ambitions to grow up to 'reach for the stars', as if the television programme *Cosmos* was a close cousin of *Star Search* and *Britain's Got Talent*.

National Expectations

Carl Sagan sold scientific grandeur extremely well partly because he was a very likable gentleman who was talking about things he was passionate about. Everyone enjoys hearing a person speak honestly about things they're in love with. Carl Sagan was in love with the material universe, and that material universe included his fellow man (or at least the material bodies of his fellow man). Therefore, he captivated his audience, some of whom didn't care two hoots about science, but they cared about Carl Sagan's passion for his work.

Most of my adult career has been spent managing construction materials laboratories, calibrating laboratory equipment, and performing research on a daily basis. I've developed conversion factors for new scales, mathematically defined a constant observation that the hot mixed asphalt industry has been repeatedly observing for many decades now. I researched the relationship between dense graded materials' particle size distributions' relationship to laboratory-prepared specimens' density and the density our paving contractors actually achieved in the real world where they were paving roads to meet tight density specifications. I know science, utilize science, and appreciate science.

But today we don't need science so much as we need to understand the opportunity costs we and our children pay when we focus so heavily on scientific education rather than balanced education (a classical education).

Carl Sagan played a role in ending the Cold War by leading American children towards science and technology. Unfortunately, that move pushed Western societies one step further into the intellectual evolution of today's Woke ideology.

The Woke ideology of today is an extreme ideology (a dual ideology) that has some schoolteachers telling young children in their classrooms to deny biological realities.

In tandem with television series about materialism and science, prime-time special documentaries captured people's attention by presenting science and materialism with all of the bells, whistles, and trappings which any 'I'm more intelligent than you' ideology could ever hope for.

Altogether these programmes were Nietzsche's emptiness filled up with data, wonderful motion-picture graphics, and articulate, likeable hosts. In Carl Sagan's case, his tone and use of repetition were hypnotic while he described to his audience a materialistic view of wonder, fantastic telescopes, interesting biographies of famous scientists, and billions and billions and billions of this or that, and little else.

That particular sort of 'filling up on material things' can be termed a Saganian tweak of Nietzsche's nihilism. It was Nietzsche's empty box, but full of so much stuff that it was easy for some people to forget that it had no soul.

Regardless of whether we use terms such as *Saganian Tweak* or other terms to describe science broadcasts' marketing of materialism, it sold popularly to the Western public until the 2000s when many Westerners didn't care to learn about science so much as they just wanted to carry its fruit in their pocket.

That fruit was the smart phone. Smart phone users didn't need to know anything about natural science or even basic arithmetic in order to use their smart phones. Instead, they only needed to remember which button did what, how to take 'selfies', and how to work the system.

That was a swing away from real science, core logic, and universal constants which are not mere computer programmes but instead are universal constants such as those that keep the four seasons and keep planets from being pulled into the Sun or drifting away into the cold of deep space.

The internet's original engineers, technology entrepreneurs, financial investment managers, and non-existent government regulations placed Western teenagers and young adults into an addictive social space where their main goal was friendship and personal growth, while social media moguls' main goal was to build, build, build.

National Expectations

While politicians were telling Westerners that everyone was going to get rich from the internet, some young people became internet junkies (addicts).

Those internet junkies became highly skilled at navigating the buttons on their monkey-see-monkey-do electronic devices, but that coincided with a weakening of their ability to understand and cope with real-world issues and direct human-to-human interactions.

Into that emotionally disconnected population of young Western people, some socio-politically active people (Marxists and globalists mostly) did something cruel.

Many cruel things were done to young people during the late 2000's while popular culture influencers were sending the message that the internet was going to improve everyone's lives. I'll pick just one cruel moment to use here as a benchmark. That benchmark was February 2009, when Mr. (redacted) made a speech to school-aged children and young people in Washington DC around the time of US President Barack Obama's 2009 presidential inauguration.

Mr. (redacted's) speech was supposed to be about 'global warming'. However, his speech was not about global warming so much as being a preacher's anxiety-filled sermon about collectivism.

Thoughtful parents who attended that event in 2009 could see that Mr. (redacted) had practically taken Karl Marx's rallying cry 'Workers of The World Unite!' and turned it into the Social-Marxist cry 'Children of The World Unite!'

Many parents who watched or attended that sermon (speech) were horrified to see and hear Mr. (redacted) essentially telling children in the audience that their parents were idiots who shouldn't be listened to.

That public display of anti-parent, anti-family, collectivist propaganda caused some responsible parents to begin a campaign against the child-manipulation techniques that activists such as Mr. (redacted) utilize.

National Expectations

After that benchmark cruel moment occurred in February of 2009, some responsible parents caused the global network of collectivists to lose a portion of their target audience (Western children).

Nonetheless, the global-climate panic movement went full steam ahead in a Marxist manner teaching young people to undervalue themselves and other individual people for the sake of the movement's panicked collectivized goals.

That movement's victory-at-all-costs tactics resulted in some young people mentally aligning their worldview with the climate-panic movement's darkly painted vision of the real world being a place where liars head Western households, and that your carbon footprint means more than you do.

After climate alarmists introduced Western young people to nihilism in that cruel way, some of those young people began an extreme rebellion against that movement's collectivist (Marxist) aspects which devalued individual human beings.

That extreme rebellion has taken global warming's communal ideology, which suggested that no person really matters, and flipped it into today's Woke crowd who tend to believe that every person's everything matters.

This kneejerk Woke rebellion is a new twist on Marxism.

I can't blame young people in general for getting caught up in it. I'm sure that some of those young people thought their only option other than this Woke rebellion was for them to surrender their individual value and identity over to socio-political global collectivists.

Today's Woke rebellion has communal foundations, but its ends are bent back on itself by way of that Progressive movement consisting of two ideologies in one larger socio-political entity.

The Woke crowd's dual ideologies have formed this basic 'Woke' ethos:

National Expectations

1. Every human being's perspective is a source of universal truth.

2. Any one person's confusion ought to be confusion shared by everyone else in society.

3. Every Woke person's personal ambitions ought to be aided by everyone around them.

4. Everyone needs to 'have a conversation' about everything, including face-to-face conversations between Woke public schoolteachers and schoolchildren about each child's sexuality and psychological matters such as the child's identity.

In some Western primary schools Woke teachers and school administrators use face-to-face conversations, Woke books, and other Woke tools for advancing the public school children towards mentally dangerous ideas such as gender fluidity (confusion), and identity fluidity (insanity).

Today those Woke teachers and their socio-political activists teach children to think that personality disorders are healthy and should be embraced by schools, children, and their parents.

This mental health issue is worse in California because during August 2025 the State of California filed a particularly problematic lawsuit against a local school district. The State of California (the State's Attorney General's Office) wants a state-wide policy that prohibits parents from being informed about their child's mental health issues displayed during school hours. That policy gives schoolteachers legal authority to manoeuvre children into living secret double lives by those children having one gender and set of pronouns at school while lying to their parents at home about it. In that way, The State of California is pushing a social agenda that attempts to teach children to lie, to lead secret double lives, and to accept personality disorders and identity fluidity as a healthy alternative to sanity.

As for older Western children and young adults in the 'Woke' crowd, they have tried to alleviate the worst psychological problems of Marxism (the loss of a sense of self) by countering it with the

National Expectations

worst opposite. That opposite thing is nothing I've noted throughout my limited studies of ancient and modern secular history.

By identifying this Woke movement's ethos as I laid out for you above, I can estimate that the spirit of this thing is something like the spirit who said, 'We are Many' and 'Legion'.

Refer to the New Testament for more information about 'Legion' and the spirit who said, 'We are Many.'

That description of the Woke movement's heart is somewhat vague in modern times. A less vague description is that it's something like Johnny Rotten's Doppelganger: Johnny Rotten wearing a lady's evening gown and boxing gloves while he demands that you tell him your life experiences, your plans for saving the world, and what your preferred pronouns are so that he doesn't risk offending you while he judges you.

And why shouldn't he, she or they judge you? After all, we're all materialists now (sarcasm).

National Expectations

Carbon footprints mean more than people do, don't they?

Generation after generation of Westerners have been taught that we're all just material objects: billions and billions and billions of objects and nothing more.

It's no wonder why it seems that today some people in the Woke crowd feel as if they're not valued in the same way that emotionally healthy people understand their intrinsic eternal value to be.

This is just my experienced opinion, but the way I see each person's intrinsic eternal value is based on the undeniable fact that every person on this planet is as rare as every other person. Logically, one-of-a-kind things (human beings in this case) are irreplaceable. Some of the victims who got sucked up into the Woke movement don't know that they have been as rare and irreplaceable as everyone else ever since before they were born.

National Expectations

Without understanding one's own intrinsic value (*that eternal value which is a constant unchanging part of each individual person*) people will look elsewhere in order to feel as valuable as any human being has the right to feel. That's one of the main causes of the Woke rebellion that the Western world is suffering from, and nowhere more so than in the very large population of parents and schoolchildren in the State of California.

One can feel sympathy for people in the Woke community. People can also feel sympathy for a person who's flailing dangerously around a crowded public pavement because they're out of their minds, weeping, anguished, and screaming about how the world hates them. One can feel sympathy for those dangerous people. Nonetheless, sympathy is not a legitimate reason for you to jeopardize your safety or your children's safety by not distancing yourself and your loved ones from harm.

I see the legal narrative that the left-wing Woke crowd is forging by manoeuvring right-wing

National Expectations

people into by eventually legally connecting 'anti-Woke rights' to 'parental rights' and connecting parental rights to 'elective-abortion rights'. Those legal connections are almost entirely unavoidable due to the fact that in democracies public narratives tend to become legal narratives that affect court decisions and houses of legislation. Therefore, I estimate that the Woke agenda is going to play out in the Western world over the next several years with the right wing feeling as if they have won a culture war by way of asserting 'Parental Rights' while the left wing expands elective abortion clinics under 'Parental Rights'.

The left will gain everything it originally wanted (a lower population by way of elective abortion), then they very well might throw the transgender lot under the bus and sadly, the right wing will thank the left wing for doing so. That may be some years away. Nonetheless, I can already almost hear the proud voices of political compromisers sharing a moment of unity like vultures sharing road-kill.

National Expectations

Even if I'd never met any people who don't respect human beings inside or outside the womb, even then I would still have my basic observations that inform me that the right wing is going to lose this democratic legal battle because the left tends to be the socio-political puppet masters while the right tends to be the socio-political puppets.

The easiest way to avoid becoming another person's puppet is for you to stand still and be rational. However, in this Woke case, rational thought is not safe if everyone remains standing still while being immersed in Woke ideology over the internet, the Entertainment Industrial Complex, and locally by friendly-faced liars who value human rights more than they value humans.

Because standing still is not an option when it comes to the Woke movement, I suggest that you attain and maintain a safe distance from the Woke nonsense. If you are a Christian who must interact with a Woke person who you can see is asking too much from you, you would benefit from following Jesus' advice in Matthew 5:37, 'Say yes, or say no. Anything more is inviting the evil one.'

National Expectations

There is no way to have a non-confusing interaction with a confused person unless you limit your responses to yes or no. Therefore, I think that it should be obvious to nearly everyone that Jesus gives Christians extraordinarily good advice in Matthew 5:37.

I'd like to add my own two cents worth of advice for you now. First, British society should get back to the basics, and know that drastic times don't always call for drastic measures. In this Woke case, drastic times call for non-drastic measures - meaning that you don't need to start an anti-Woke rebellion against the leftist political madness that ushered in Woke ideology. In my opinion, the most reasonable approach is for you to avoid complexity.

Without too much effort, I can think of six categories of people who flourish in overly complex societies. These six are insane people, opportunists, dishonest people, immoral people, criminals, and the Woke crowd.

National Expectations

Therefore, I think that it's a very good idea for British society to avoid unnecessary complexity, get back to the basics and back to classical education which is well balanced for well-balanced minds that are capable of defending against fundamentalist ideologies such as the Woke's dual ideology.

National Expectations

Part 4 – A Classical Education

A classical education claims people's intellect away from fundamentalism and extremist viewpoints. A classical education does that effortlessly because fundamentalism and extremism are by definition unbalanced, whereas a classical education is well balanced.

Classical education is well balanced by including multiple subjects such as mathematics, literature, and music. Although I haven't covered all of those subjects in this book, I've covered a very wide range of topics in this book. And I could do that fairly easily because of a happy coincidence that occurred in AD 432 when, after landing in Dublin, Saint Patrick travelled west to or towards my family's camp in Coolderry.

Various maps of Saint Patrick's land journey are easy to find on the internet if you would like to confirm that information.

At any rate, that historical event allowed me to include in this book an 'old school' sized portion of traditional topics that are staples of a classical education.

That historical event of AD 432 has also benefited readers by allowing me to write a useful book that isn't weighted down by a complex storyline.

In fact, there is almost no storyline at all in this book. Instead of a storyline, after this first chapter the book is held together by a single court case decided in AD 432 and again in 2025.

The AD 432 court case is based on a realistic instance of Saint Patrick travelling to central Ireland to present Christianity and the Holy Bible to my British ancestor (my great, great,...grandfather) in Rose Creed, Ireland (Roscrea, Ireland), in order to get his opinion about Christianity and whether our people at home in Britain should continue being Christian after the Roman Empire fell.

That AD 432 interaction between Saint Patrick and my ancestor was essentially a court case that I've worded in this book as follows:

National Expectations

British Society with Christianity

vs.

British Society without Christianity

One of the reasons that I worded the court case in that way is that I always try to follow my moral code that tells me to do no harm; and obviously I'd have risked doing harm to Christianity if I'd worded the court case in some other way.

As the court case is worded, I risk doing little more harm to Christianity with this book than I might do to classical music if I wrote a book about why classical music is healthy for British society. That sort of book would be more about society than it would be about classical music. The same holds true for this book.

Aside from the last two chapters and this opening chapter, all of the other chapters in this book are essentially court submittals that relate to the court case.

Some of the chapters are poetry while others are modern-style essays. One chapter is very analytical and consists mostly of a logical progression. Altogether, the book is broad enough to give readers a sense of what a classical education feels like after you've had a bit of it from this book.

The last two chapters are the AD 432 and 2025 written court's opinions for the case: British Society with Christianity vs. British Society without Christianity.

I hope that while reading this book you enjoy as much courtroom suspense as you think there ought to be for such a court case.

Part 5 – Law and Mercy

There is a very important social aspect of The United Kingdom that we share with most of the other civilized Western nations. That shared aspect is that we are 'Women and Children First' societies.

I can't think of a more obvious touchstone of this humane issue than Britain's most famous memorial statue of a widow and orphans.

That memorial statue is of Queen Boudicca and her two orphaned children. Her story as told by historians was Roman propaganda that was dishonest and harmful. Nonetheless we can pull something good from the memorial statue if we have an eye for good.

That bronze memorial statue stands near the Westminster Bridge in London. It was placed there in 1902. The artist has my ancestor Queen Boudicca's hands outstretched as she faces Big Ben and the British Parliament building.

This memorial statue of Boudicca and her two orphaned children reminds some people today

National Expectations

that the first time a large democracy (Rome's Republic) existed on our island its power was used to either beat and rape native Britons or psychologically torture (terrorize) multiple native populations on the British Isles.

The bronze memorial statue can remind us of that horrible history and nothing more. Or if you care to see it from the perspective of a native parent who's more concerned for their children's future then for the past, you may also be able to see the bronze memorial statue as a steady daily reminder to every British person and visitor that our island is not a social experiment, nor is our island a courtroom, nor are our people on trial. Instead, our island is our home where there are rules and there is love, and where honest British people today can live well in a public space consisting of Law and Mercy.

2
The Rugged Road of Freedom (an old poem)

The Rugged Road of Freedom

I cannot prove all of the good things which I believe; yet, I am free to prove that I believe them.

I cannot prove that eternal life exists; yet, I can prove that I am eternally grateful for the life I have.

I cannot prove that God exists; yet, I can prove that I am small enough to need Him.

I cannot prove that we all must accept ourselves, our nations, and the world as they are; yet, I can prove that I have become more at peace after accepting these things myself.

National Expectations

I cannot prove what awaits each of us over the horizon, on the other side of freedom; but I can prove that I believe it is destiny, and that our freedom is a road, not a goal.

Destiny isn't merely tomorrow and beyond; destiny is with each of us every day. It is the people beside us, the challenges in front of us, the failures behind us, the courage in our guts, the loved ones in our hearts, the people who fill us, and the people whose absence empties us while we wait to see them again.

Every day is yesterday's horizon. Therefore, every day our feet stand, in comfort or discomfort, exactly where they ought to be, and if we wait for the bitter to pass us by, then we will discover that life is sweet.

I cannot prove these good and rugged things I believe; yet, with this life God has blessed me with, I can spend my career proving that I believe them. Then, I will do what wise men do – I will simply enjoy them.

National Expectations

We can hear God when we are still. We can see destiny when we move. And in the combination of the two, we are human, and we find our humanity along the rugged road of freedom.

Poem's End

National Expectations

3
The Parable of the Literalist

Long ago, when human beings were rare, and human intelligence was even rarer, two young women named Truth lost their respective tribes while they were separately collecting berries in the forest one morning.

Mid afternoon that day, one of the young women was walking down a hill while the other was walking up that same hill.

When the two walked close enough to speak to one another, Downhill Truth said to the other young woman, 'Hello. My name is Truth. I lost my tribe this morning while we were all collecting berries. Have you seen anyone who might be from my tribe?'

Uphill Truth replied, 'Hello. My name is also Truth. I haven't seen anyone who might be from your tribe, and I've been walking for hours because I also lost my tribe this morning. Have you seen anyone today that might be from my tribe?'

Downhill Truth responded, 'No one except for you. You are from your tribe, and I see you. But other than you, I haven't seen anyone who might be from your tribe. But, I will mention you to them if I come across anyone from your tribe. What is your tribe called?'

Uphill Truth answered, 'My tribe is called Spirit. What is your tribe called?' Downhill Truth replied, 'My tribe is called Literal.'

Uphill Truth responded, 'It's nice to meet you, Truth of Literal. I must go now and keep searching for my tribe.' Then she continued to walk up the hill. Truth of Literal then said to her, 'Truth of Spirit, I can't see through all of these trees. Will you please tell me what is at the bottom of this hill?'

Truth of Spirit answered, 'There is a stream at the bottom of this hill. I was just down there skipping rocks across the water to help myself relax a little before continuing my search for my tribe.'

Truth of Literal replied, 'Skipping stones across the water helps you relax?'

Truth of Spirit answered, 'Yes. And now that I'm relaxed, I can think more clearly and do a better job of searching for my tribe.'

Truth of Literal replied, 'I shall do the same.' Then she ran down the hill, picked up an armful of stones from the bank of the stream, and skipped across the stream until it became deep, at which time she fell into the water over her head.

Truth of Literal then swam to the bank and stepped angrily to dry ground, where she yelled up the hill to Truth of Spirit, 'That was not relaxing! You lied to me!'

Truth of Spirit replied down the hill, 'No. You did it wrong. I'll come down and show you.'

Then Truth of Spirit ran down the hill to teach Truth of Literal how to skip stones across the stream. After arriving at the bank of the stream,

Truth of Spirit picked up a flat stone and threw it low across the surface of the stream, causing it to skip across the surface of the water.

After seeing that, Truth of Literal said to Truth of Spirit, 'That stone bounced; it did not skip. Feet skip. Stones do not. You are a liar.'

Truth of Spirit replied, 'No, I am not a liar. I'll show you. I'll find a stone for you to throw. Then you might understand better.'

Truth of Spirit then bent over and began searching the ground for just the right stone for Truth of Literal's first ever throw of a skipping stone. As she did that, Truth of Literal picked up a large stone, lifted it into the air, and then lowered it quickly, smashing Truth of Spirit's skull in.

Truth of Literal then stood over Truth of Spirit's dead body and said, 'I am Truth, and I kill liars.'

End

That concludes 'The Parable of the Literalist'. It isn't my place to tell you exactly what lesson or lessons to draw from that parable. All I can respectfully suggest to you is that, whatever lessons you draw from that parable, you shouldn't take those lessons too literally.

National Expectations

4

An Explanation of the Welsh 'Sin-Eater'

Part of today's Welsh culture is the unique tradition of a 'sin-eater' attending some traditional Welsh funerals. What I'm about to write to you explains how that tradition evolved over thousands of years ago.

When Welsh society was originally forming thousands of years ago, the Welsh people considered how best to get along with one another. They understood that friendships caused biased opinions and biased judgments; therefore, the ancient Welsh (who called themselves Cymry) decided to ban one of their members to the forest. This member was to remain friendless, and therefore unbiased and useful as a reliable judge who could be called out of the forest whenever the ancient Welsh needed to hold court on an important case.

The lonely Welsh judge who was banished to the forest was not allowed to interact with people (unless court was in session), nor were people allowed to interact with him unless court was in session.

While living all alone in the forest, this lonely unbiased judge might have starved to death if not for the kindness of the Welsh people who would sometimes leave food for him at the edge of the forest. Because gratitude can create bias, the banished Welsh judge was not allowed to see or thank the Welsh person who was leaving food for him. Therefore, taking food to the ostracized judge was literally a thankless task, and therefore somewhat selfless.

With the human psyche being as it is, ancient individual Welsh people noticed that they felt better after doing the thankless task of leaving food at the edge of the wood for the ostracized judge. And so, the act of leaving food for the judge had the psychological effect of atonement. And so, when an ancient Welsh person felt bad about something they had done and they couldn't set it right in some other manner, they'd deliver food to the edge of the forest for the ostracized judge. Then they'd feel better.

When Christianity arrived in Wales, these acts of atonement were no longer necessary. However, unbiased judgements were still occasionally required. Therefore, the judges remained ostracized, living in the forests of Wales. A judge risked death if not for the kindness of the Welsh who left food for him to eat so he wouldn't starve to death while doing his job of being the Welsh people's unbiased, friendless judge.

Some centuries later, the Normans stormed into Wales, built the highest concentration of castles on the planet, subdued the Welsh people, and enforced Norman law on the land. At this time, the ostracized judges no longer served a legally practical purpose, and the number of ostracized judges in Wales dropped. Nonetheless, in some smaller Welsh communities, the act of leaving food for the ostracized judge had become an important part of Welsh society's psychological wellbeing. As such, some of these small Welsh communities continued to have ostracized Welshmen in the forests.

Some Welsh people continued that tradition of keeping a sin-eater long enough into our recent past that they carried it into the Appalachian Mountains, where the tradition continued to provide the mental-health benefit of doing a good deed.

Now, in modern times, you might think that there are lots of places where a person can do someone a kindness and not be thanked in return. However, I assure you that it was harder in past generations to do that than it is today. Today you can invite a person over to your house for dinner, and they may not return your kindness by inviting you to their house for dinner in order to repay your generosity. However, in past generations, almost no one would accept a favour (such as being fed a meal) without repaying that favour.

National Expectations

A good deed that is repaid with a good deed doesn't have the same healthy psychological benefit as does doing a good deed for absolutely nothing in return. When one receives nothing in return for their good deed, it is selfless and psychologically beneficial to the giver and receiver. When the Welsh stopped keeping judges confined in the forests, the Welsh lost an avenue for charitable anonymity for centuries until it redeveloped with urbanization that brought needy people into the cities.

There in the cities, charitable contributions could be made to feed, clothe, and shelter the needy, who could never thank you for your kindness, because they didn't know you.

After modern methods of charity that included anonymous giving became available, the Welsh tradition of having a sin-eater became what it is today: something limited to funerals, where most of the people in attendance understand that it's for the sake of maintaining the Welsh people's historical memory, and not for reasons that conflict with Christian doctrine.

National Expectations

In order to keep this book short, I'll keep this chapter short by just mentioning that this particular Welsh tradition reminds us in our time that at least some humans have historically always sought unbiased rulings: humans have historically understood that some people had to make unique sacrifices that other people in their society didn't have to make; and what ancient Welsh history also tells us is that at least some ancient people understood that one's wellbeing is benefitted when they complete an anonymous act of kindness for which they expect nothing in return.

5
Practical History

Most Westerners today compile history books full of accurate names, dates, and events; then they hand those history books to their children and say to them, 'This is what has happened so far.'

In contrast to that, Western people many hundreds (and thousands) of years ago recorded our history as story from oral histories. Our oral histories were full of lessons rather than superfluous details. Because we recorded and taught lessons instead of mere dates and names, when we handed our children a lesson in history, we taught life-lessons. And instead of handing our children a book and saying, 'This is what has happened thus far,' Western people used to hand our children a rich oral history and say to them, 'This is what our people have learned thus far.'

Unlike our old Western ways of teaching history, the modern way of teaching history in most Western countries today allows recorded names and groups of people to become the targets of ridicule, and it causes historical events to be 'reimagined' or rewritten. That leaves the truly valuable lessons of history to be unprotected putty, from which modern opportunists mould narratives in order to support their preferred lessons, which don't exist except in those opportunists' heads.

Historic details don't help your children as much as historic lessons do. That's why our old Western oral histories can be characterized as 'practical history'. I use the word 'practical' here because historical lessons have practical use today, whereas historical details generally don't have any practical use today.

Due to the fact that in my fabled predecessor's time (AD 432), our people would have been used to focusing on historical lessons rather than on details, my predecessor would have seen the Holy Bible as a wealth of important lessons and not just

National Expectations

a book full of details. British people's oral history of centuries ago as well as other nations' oral histories and the stories of the Holy Bible are all sources of practical history. Yet, only the Holy Bible bridges national, ethnic, and cultural divides.

The Holy Bible contains immeasurably valuable lessons. Therefore, the ancients in their time, me in my time, and you in your time, would be beyond foolish if we were to abandon this most valuable of all books ever written, the Holy Bible.

National Expectations

6
Absolute History

History books tend to be filled with dates and events, but little or nothing about what was truly going on in the hearts and minds of the people who lived through the history about which history books educate people. Therefore, you have to understand that when you look at history merely as a set of dates and events, one leading to the next as if the world were not much more than the product of inevitable cause and effect relationships, you might become prone to attempt to do good in the world by using the things around you instead of what is inside you.

If you wait for events that you can take advantage of, you will be allowing circumstances rather than God to chart your course. So, if you want God instead of mere circumstances as your guide, then you have to be careful about how you

National Expectations

read history and how you apply history to your decision-making today.

History will not tell you the difference between right and wrong, but God does. Therefore, you should be aware that when you study history books as a mere series of cause-and-effect events, you can be led to point the finger of blame at one group of people or another. However, if we examine history – not to find dates, names, and blame, but instead to find truth – we can peer back into time to before history was written, back to the first Britons, and even further back still to the beginning that is common to all human beings. We know few details about the occurrences in that very ancient time, yet we know there is a story there because everything tells a story.

Logic dictates that every story is either a love story or it is not. If our earliest common history was not a love story, then perhaps no human being has ever mattered, nor will ever truly matter. However, if our earliest history was a love story, then every human being always matters, and to live a love story in one's own life is a prerequisite to leading a fully honest life.

National Expectations

7
A Human Condition

All humans share a common experience. Some people call it 'the human condition'. It's common to us no matter our position on the globe or our position in our societies. Different philosophers have their differing notions as to exactly what the human condition is.

I'm not looking for a fight with philosophers. Therefore I'll not tell you that I'm here to discuss *the* human condition, but merely *a* common human condition, which is this: we come to life without any effort of our own, and then manage our way through gestation and leave the warm comfort of the womb to live in the bright lights and busy sounds of everyday life. We all share that same experience and the same circumstance of being in possession of a life that we know we could not have created ourselves, for you can't go back in time to before you were created and create

National Expectations

yourself. It requires a person's wilful ignorance for them to avoid discussing the fact that none of us could have possibly earned or caused our initial moment of life, for before that moment we didn't exist, and after that moment we were alive.

Because we know it defies reason that anyone could earn or cause their first moments of life, we know that we're in debt to God for our existence. However, we don't all approach that debt in the same way. Some of you even ignore your obvious debt. It's not a typical debt of money, but regardless of your debt's uniqueness, we know that, for a lack of good reason to consider our obvious debt false, we must consider our obvious debt true and legitimate.

I'll here address you directly, dear reader, so I don't word this chapter in such a way that it's made easy for you to point at another, without looking at yourself in the mirror. That now explained, I tell you that I understand this may be the first time you have considered this debt, but I assure you that the obviousness of the debt has not escaped the back of your mind, for your debt is as obvious as your own existence. Of course, this topic ties into religious topics, so I hope that every reader appreciates my self-discipline in avoiding the religious aspects of this topic, considering that I do so for the broader audience of this book. The human condition is common to us all.

After you become aware of your debt, the next reasonable question is, if I could not possibly have earned or caused my initial moments of life, who paid, or by what mechanism or reasoning did I come into being?

We know that questions regarding the creation of the entire material universe preclude us from assuming that any material thing could have prompted it, so we form the following question: I could not have possibly earned or caused my first moments of life – humans know of no just cause for our creation – so then, what reasoning causes something (life, matter) to be given without just cause?

In one's search for an answer, you will find that the only non-material thing we're aware of that acts without just cause is love. Love is exclusive of all other non-material things because it's the only thing that can be understood as purely selfless.

Logic that leads to love is an unfamiliar logic for most of you. However, for some of you it's glorious. In either case, logical answers are not measured by their familiarity to us, or by their personal usefulness to us, or by their beauty: logic is logic whether we like it or not. If you are uncomfortable with the word love, you can use the synonym selfless.

We've never observed a rock loving anything, so our observations lead us to limit the emotion of love to beings. Considering that mankind's consensus view is that love is not exhibited by beings that don't have personality, the consensus conclusion ought to be that the love that initiated creation (our lives) came from a being with personality.

In consideration of the previous paragraphs, I think that you can see that, although the human condition is one of inherent debt, logic results in the same conclusion that most religions around the world believe – a being created the universe and everything in it including you and me. I'd be insulting your intelligence if I completely ignored the obvious similarity between logic's conclusion of a loving creator God and the God written about in the New Testament.

In summary of this chapter, the human condition is a matter of fact, regardless of whether or not the facts sound poetic, align with a particular religion, or appear too good to be true. Facts are facts. If you doubt the logic, clear your mind of preconceived notions and superfluous information, then reread this chapter and accept the facts as they are.

The human condition can be summarized this way. The human condition is that we're inherently loved by our creator, and we may either unjustly act as thieves ignoring our debt, or we can justly reciprocate His love.

In human dealings, debts are a matter of contract (verbal or written). Therefore, the

National Expectations

situation of having come to life under a debt you didn't agree to may seem like an unjust situation to some people. However, creation and life could be no other way. You see, the human condition is a beautiful necessity.

In logical terms, the beauty of our human condition ought not to be noted here, because beauty is not a qualifier of a strictly logical conclusion. Yet, as someone with a heart, I must for a moment set aside the strict discipline of hard, cold logic and tell you that in all my years of meditating and drawing conclusions on important topics, I've found that when reason or logic leads us to understand a deep truth, we're unavoidably emotionally moved. That emotional response is part of having a healthy human heart. If you enjoy the beauty of our debt of love, please still your enjoyment before you begin reading the next chapter, because in the next chapter we're on to a logical examination of the seemingly apparent unfairness that this chapter has mentioned.

8
The Unfairness Confusion

In the previous chapter we discovered the inherent debt of our existence. That idea of inherent debt is foreign to most people, who typically enter into debt by mutual consent. The previous chapter also contradicts human standard notions about fairness. Therefore, some people may be asking 'Is this inherent debt (for our creation) fair?'

Most honest and logical people will quickly conclude that because the debt is inherent it's fair, because inherent things are inherently fair. For instance, when you throw a ball up into the air, the ball will inherently come back down. No one considers that inherent situation to be unfair, nor do they consider it unfair when spring turns to summer or fall becomes winter. Those are

National Expectations

inherent things and inherently fair. Our inherent debt is as fair as a cloud inherently becoming rain or a river inherently changing course over time. You don't need to be a genius to understand that inherent things are inherently fair; however, you do need to be honest in order to accept it. Honest, logical people don't need to read the remainder of this chapter because you already understand. But, as there may be a dishonest person reading this book, I've included the remainder of this chapter in hopes that they may surrender to the simple truths about the inherent fairness of this debt of love: this human condition that all humans share.

Everyone ought to know that a seemingly logical question is not worth perusing if all possible answers are of no use for improving understanding, or if the answer will not have an honest application. The point that I'm getting at is that our personal conclusions to the question of our inherent debt's fairness are of no consequence because, regardless of our personal notions regarding fairness, the debt still exists.

National Expectations

If a person can bend their mind far enough to reason that the debt is unfair, they can falsely justify ignoring their debt, and that's dishonest. Everyone knows that it's a dishonest act to attempt to wiggle out of a debt by unilaterally applying your own terms (your notions of fairness). Considering that you don't talk to the Creator, the big bang, or whatever you attribute our creation to, you have no way of receiving mutual agreement to your terms, and therefore you may offer no new deal. There is only one deal, and it's common to us all. Whether you like it or not, that's fair by all reasonable people's standards.

I think that most of you readers can now understand that our situation (human existence, this human condition we all share) is indeed fair. Nonetheless, I'll write just a few more points here in order to be as fair as I can be to everyone who reads this book.

Over many years the term 'fairness' has been specified and re-specified by the laws and customs of various cultures. Additionally, the term

National Expectations

'fairness' has been redefined by each of you when you set your expectations for what life within your society ought to be. Our hopes and dreams can lead us to set our expectations too high. Anyone can hope for a world free of disease, 500-year earthly lifespans, and rainbows every morning just after breakfast, but only fools expect those things and then cry foul when they don't get what they expected out of life. You may not have expected to owe a debt for creation, but you do. And you can't avoid the debt in any manner, including by considering the debt to be unfair or unexpected.

9
Romance

Love is blind. That's a very well-known saying partly because of its insightfulness and partly because it gives a practical warning to people who may be blinded by love. I assert that love is not inherently or inescapably blind, but rather that this particular blindness is brought on by the person who is in love and who intentionally blinds their senses to their love's flaws in order to feel a greater sense of awe and justification for the love they feel. That understood, we can now also understand that when a person does something reckless or self-defiling and claims that they did it solely because they were carried away by romantic love, that reckless person actually carried themselves away. Truly, love is a legitimate reason for good behaviour and never a legitimate excuse for bad behaviour.

National Expectations

If people can dishonestly excuse their reckless behaviour by accounting it to their love for another person, we ought to be concerned about the practice that is termed by New Age thinkers and spiritualists of various kinds as 'self-love'.

The modern focus on self-love began during the last several decades with pop culture movements towards self-serving spirituality and New Age philosophies. Certainly, some people who loathe themselves are benefitted by being aware of good reasons to respect themselves, but respect (*and the forgiveness that respect usually requires*) is not love. Respect and forgiveness don't blind a person, yet love very often does. So then, in the generations of people who have been taught to love themselves first, a crucial question is, 'What does self-love blind a person to?'

The answer is that self-love blinds (*or has a great capacity to blind*) a person to their own flaws. It also blinds them to accurate understandings of everyone else, the world around them, and the true mysteries of life. In that social-wide psychosis, the self-loving (self-centred) person finds the greatest reasons for loving themselves when they not only blind themselves to their own flaws, but when they also blind themselves to other people's goodness. The self-centred person finds increased justification for their spiritually isolated self-love (self-centredness) with every neighbour, family member, classical hero, noble institution, and orthodoxy that they can tear down or see in a poor light. They (*and no one else*) are their own chosen one true love. Their stance and no one else's is the correct stance. Their political views, and no one else's, are correct. Such is self-love's blinding nature.

With all that understood, you readers ought to understand that, along with other self-centred social forces, self-love killed true romance in the modern world. Not only did the overgrown self-love movement kill (*or more accurately, injure*) the true romance between husbands and wives or fiancés and fiancées; it also very much wounded the platonic love that our cultures used to be romantic about and which closely unites people to their families, neighbourhoods, nations, church, and God.

Self-love, selfishness, the greed so popularized by radio talk-show hosts, the materialism promoted in much of mainstream films and lyrical music – these are all currently dragging humanity down. Numerous terror attacks, frequently violent political demonstrations, destabilized economic markets, venomous political speech, and general divisiveness in Western democratic societies make most people very aware that we have a problem. In a basic sense, that problem is that most people blame everyone but themselves for all the current troubles that comprise humanity's troubles.

The solution will not be found in politics, trade agreements, or modern technology. The solution will not be found in the new socio-political orthodoxy that has been forming for the last centuries. That modern socio-political orthodoxy can be described as secular-impulsiveness, lowest-common-denominator governance, politics-as-usual.

National Expectations

Neither that modern socio-political orthodoxy (*secular impulsiveness, politics as usual, etc.*), nor the self-love that permeates it, will solve today's larger problems or save humanity. Now, regardless of how little you may esteem humanity, I hope that you understand that today's many problems stem from people forgetting their humanity or never being taught their humanity in the first place.

If you want to save humanity, trade in your self-love for self-respect and personal dignity. If you want to save humanity, be a romantic: selfless, chivalrous, virtuous, yielding to God, and demonstrating other good character traits. If you want to save humanity, save your energy from the sword swung or pen scribed in hopes of changing the world. For though the pen is mightier than the sword, neither is required where there is compassion.

National Expectations

10

The One and Only Certainty

Dear reader, this chapter is the chapter I was referring to earlier in this book when I stated that I'd written one perhaps overly analytical chapter for anal-retentive, humourless fellows such as me. If you don't enjoy over-thinking things, you may choose to skip this chapter. I won't be a bit offended if you do. However, if you care to venture down the wordy path of people who have too much time on their hands, you can do that here in this chapter.

In order for an idea or statement to be considered as capital 't' True, people correctly expect that idea or statement to stand on some correct assumption that supports whatever the idea or statement is that is considered to be capital 't' True. That's common sense, as well as basic logic.

When one considers that every genuinely true statement must be supported by some genuinely true underlying idea or statement, a picture emerges and the basic structure of logic begins to reveal itself.

When one considers that no two seemingly unrelated ideas or statements can be supported by two different assumptions that contradict one another, one can see that there are fewer fundamental truths (supportive truths) than there are truths that are supported by those fundamental truths. For instance, the fundamental truth that *the Cleveland Browns are not going to win the Super Bowl this football season* is a single fundamental truth that supports many less-fundamental truths such as the true statement that no Cleveland Browns' player will win the Super Bowl MVP (Most Valuable Player award) this season, nor will *Sports Illustrated* magazine be featuring a picture of the Cleveland Browns head coach holding the Super Bowl trophy

National Expectations

on the cover of their magazine this season. In this light-hearted example of how logic is structured, you can understand that one underlying truth regarding this season's Super Bowl championship game supports several other less-fundamental truths.

What I just described about logic's structure is simple enough that I think you can understand that the deeper a philosopher or logician delves into the entirety of logic the fewer and fewer underlying truths there are at each layer. If one dives deep enough, one will eventually reach the one certain truth that supports all other genuine truths.

One of the reasons that I thought this enquiry into logic's deepest level was worthy of going down intellectually is that some people consider themselves to be too logical for faith of any sort. They may believe that science, calculations, and logic alone will save the world. Therefore, to some extent, logic is to them their messiah or god. I figured this was worth including in this difficult-to-read chapter so the people who believe that they're too logical for Christian faith (too logical to be saved by Grace and Mercy) could meet their exclusively logical God face-to-face, or at least get a sense of what that logical meeting would be like.

This chapter is that intellectual journey, that logical meeting, and a bit more.

Identifying the one central certainty that lies at the heart or bottom level of logic requires one to examine a presumably true statement's underlying assumption (its supportive assumed truth) and then to repeat that process at each deeper level one arrives at intellectually.

This process of getting to the core of logic requires a process that relies on the same three fundamental laws of logic that all logicians rely on. The three fundamental laws of logic are:

1. The law of *identity*: P is P.

2. The law of *non-contradiction*: P is not non-P.

3. The law of the *excluded middle*:

        Either P or non-P.

National Expectations

I'll do my best to adhere to those laws of logic as I write this chapter for the hyper-logically minded reader. I'll begin this chapter's logical progression (a search for The One and Only Certainty) with the idea of freewill, because many people who think that they're too logical for Christianity think of themselves that way because Christianity presumes each person is responsible for their own actions. It's important to note here that if a person wants to bail out of their responsibility for their own actions, one way to do that is to deny that Christianity serves any purpose. Another way to bail out is for that person to vehemently deny that freewill exists.

One of the problems with investigating whether or not freewill exists is a problem that rests on the fact that everyone is heavily invested in the answer. Much hangs in the balance for everyone if someone proves that freewill doesn't exist. For instance, if freewill doesn't exist, then no one is actually guilty of any crime. So, if someone were to rape and murder you, it wouldn't be logical for you to dislike that person because, after all, supposedly they have no freewill by which they could chose to do anything other than to commit their crimes against you. Additionally, after you were murdered, no one could logically hold your murderer accountable for his or her actions. Therefore, if science, philosophy, or some other field of human endeavour ever 'proves' (small p) that freewill doesn't exist, then everyone will have to chalk cruelty up to some imaginary puppet strings that are supposedly controlling everyone's actions in the complete absence of freewill.

So, I think that you can understand that anyone who promotes the idea that freewill doesn't exist, is a person who promotes the abolition of personal responsibility. And because personal responsibility is one of the key components of a civilized society, as well as your local and national security, you might understand that the promotion of the idea that freewill doesn't exist, unavoidably promotes anarchy (lawlessness) and whatever inhumanities arise from it.

Fortunately for me and you, dear reader, both answers regarding freewill stand on the same underlying assumption. Therefore, we don't have to split hairs about freewill's existence in order to move this chapter along. So, let's get started by comparing the two basic statements regarding freewill. Then we'll examine those statements' supporting assumptions. The two statements we'll be comparing are:

1. I have freewill.

2. I do not have freewill.

We can't yet ask ourselves which of those statements is true and which statement is false, because both statements rest on the assumption that the word 'I' in each statement is a real thing. Therefore, the next logical step in this downward progression is for us to compare two opposing statements, which are:

1. I am real.

2. I am not real.

To decide whether statement 1 or statement 2 is correct, we must examine ourselves as individual people. In my examinations I've noticed that we each can observe and control our bodies, but we're not our bodies. We observe, judge, and control our emotions (in some cases), but we're not our emotions. We observe reality with our eyes, ears, touch, and logic, yet we're not our eyes, ears, touch, or logic. The common thread in all of those instances is that we're always the observer, and we judge what we may judge and we control what we may control.

Therefore, a logical definition of ourselves must be very similar to the awkwardly defined 'observer who sometimes judges and who sometimes controls particular things'. A much more common definition is that we're souls. You may use either the awkward or the common definition: it makes no difference to this logical progression.

Now that we've defined the 'I' of our statement, we can answer our question about whether or not we're real. We can begin that by admitting that we are 'observers who . . .' Well, obviously an observer is a thing, a real thing. Therefore we must conclude this truth:

National Expectations

Truth: I am real. (I'm a soul.) (I'm the observer who sometimes...)

Next...

The supporting idea (assumption) of the statement 'I am real' is the assumption that reality is real. The inverse of that statement is the statement 'Reality is not real.'

That leaves us with these two opposing statements:

1. Reality is real.

2. Reality is not real (or reality is an illusion).

Believe it or not dear reader, some philosophers disagree with statement 1. Fortunately those philosophers' mistaken opinions are of little consequence because Statement 2 breaks the first law of logic, which is called The Law of Identity: the law of logic that states that P is P.

Statement 2 breaks that law of logic. However, statement 1 doesn't break any laws of logic. Therefore, the only strictly logical conclusion is that statement 1 is correct. That leaves me to write the extraordinarily obvious true statement:

Truth: Reality is real.

Next...

The statement 'Reality is real' is a self-supporting statement. That is to say that that statement's supporting ideas (assumptions) are contained within the statement itself, as if to state 'facts are facts', or 'reality is reality', or 'P is P'.

Our last true statement, 'Reality is real,' is a self-supporting statement. Therefore, we're left only to dig deeper in order to see what we may learn about this thing we call reality.

By digging deeper, the reasonable question that many of you would ask about reality is, 'Did reality have a beginning?' That isn't the same as asking, 'Did the material universe have a beginning?' Questions regarding the material universe are questions for physicists to theorize about and measure. Physicists are trained in observing and measuring (as accurately as they currently can) observable and measurable things:

the material universe. Physicists are not trained in answering questions such as why physics exists, or whether consciousness is separate or inseparable from the material world.

If I'm going to expect physicists not to overstep their academic jurisdiction, I shall have to return that respect by keeping my remarks within this chapter's jurisdiction, which is limited to logic. That is why I'm limited in this chapter to commenting on reality and not the material universe.

This disciplined approach leaves me to compare two opposing statements, which are:

1. Reality had a beginning.

2. Reality did not have a beginning.

If reality had no beginning, then infinity already exists in our past. If that statement sounds irrational to you then you are in good company because mathematicians' consensus view of the concept of infinity is that infinity is irrational and an 'unreal' number. That's what the mathematicians generally say, and I agree with them because infinity is unobservable as well as immeasurable. Logic doesn't allow a legitimate logician to professionally consider unobservable things. Therefore, academic discipline requires me to conclude that reality had a beginning, and to write this conclusion in a somewhat formal manner such as I've been doing so far in this chapter, which is:

Truth: Reality had a beginning.

A beginning requires a creation, and the idea of creation leads us to contrast and compare the two following statements:

1. The beginning happened with a creation.

2. The beginning happened without a creation.

Dear reader, if you would like to find some wiggle room for the point in this chapter, you can call your attorneys and ask them for the legally defined difference between the words 'beginning' and 'creation'. Or you can save yourself the legal fees and just concede that beginnings and creations are essentially indistinguishable from one another due to the fact that beginnings and creations always coincide. Therefore, the words 'beginning' and 'creation' are synonymous and inseparable. Therefore, statement 2 breaks the first law of logic, which is the Law of Identity: P is P.

Now with statement 2 falsified, deductive reasoning leaves us to conclude:

Truth: The beginning happened with a creation

Next…

Considering that we've just concluded that reality began with a creation (obviously), I think that the most basic next question is whether or not creation was accidental or intentional. Here we compare these two opposing statements:

1. Creation was intentional.

2. Creation was an accident.

If we're going to start this comparison by examining statement 1, we'll have to define what sort of intention was involved in creation. Therefore, we may be putting the cart before the horse if we examine statement 1 first. So, let's examine statement 2 first.

Statement 2 states that creation happened by accident. By definition, an accident requires something to do something contrary to what it was expected to do or intended to do. Therefore, the expectation or intention must exist prior to the action, reaction, or occurrence to which you are trying to apply the term 'accident'. Therefore, the earliest possible moment of any accident occurring is sometime after creation has occurred.

Occurrences that we consider to be accidents do exist. However, they could not have logically occurred at the moment of creation. Therefore, we must conclude that creation was an intentional occurrence, and that it could not possibly have been the result of an accident. Therefore, the conclusion at this step is:

Truth: Creation was intentional.

Next...

Our conclusion that creation was intentional raises the question 'What is an intention?'

We've never observed the material form of an intention. Therefore, we categorize intentions as something akin to emotions – things that prompt actions in the material world but are not material themselves.

We've never observed a rock or any other non-living thing with intentions or emotions. Nor have we ever observed an intention or emotion existing without its originating from a person or being. Therefore, the evidence leads us to conclude that the intention that caused the beginning originated from a being, person, or the common component of those two. That common component is 'personality'.

Therefore, the Creator has personality and can logically be termed 'God', as we moderns are familiar with the term God.

The next question in this logical progression would be, 'What was God's intention or emotion during creation?' However, no one can comment on any 'intentions' in this instance because to do so would be to claim that you know God's plan, for intentions are essentially the same as plans. So, instead of asking a disrespectful question regarding God's intention, I'll merely ask the safer question 'What was the emotion present at the moment of creation?'

Aside from one specific emotion, all other emotions require other things. For example, sorrow requires loss, hate requires something to hate, anger requires something to be angry about, pain requires injury, joy requires something to be joyful about, happiness requires circumstance, frustration requires expectation, and so on. Dear reader, the only thing that can exist on its own is the only selfless thing we human beings are aware of: love.

Now considering that creation was an action, we can attempt to examine the next-to-last two opposing statements:

1. God created as an act of love.

2. No option; the previous paragraph already ruled out all possible opposing statements.

So, we're left with no logical option other than to conclude:

Truth: God created as an act of love.

Next…

Forming the next question, we know that the true statement 'God created as an act of love' was logically concluded and that no other logical options exist. But do you doubt it? Are you uncertain of it?

Those questions regarding one's certainty are the only sorts of questions remaining to be asked in this logical progression. So, let's ask in the same logical manner of contrasting and comparing two opposing statements:

1. I am certain God created as an act of love.

2. I am uncertain that God created as an act of love. Or, I doubt that God created as an act of love. Or, I doubt God. - *It makes no logical difference which way you choose to word it, because the intention of those various wordings is the same intention.*

Now, I'll go out on a limb here to suggest that a large portion of readers will choose option 1 listed above. That option was the statement 'I am certain God created as an act of love.' So, let's explore that option for a moment.

Truth: I am certain God created as an act of love.

Well, that's not a statement regarding love in general, nor is that statement about your certainty about yourself. Instead, it's a statement about your certainty in the one who, in that previous statement, loves: the Creator, God.

What I mean there is that the most fundamental truth (the One and Only Certainty) is not certainty itself, but rather the personality behind the certainty of our last logical statement, which, according to this logical progression thus far can identify, is the deepest root of every truly logical statement that will ever be.

That personality is, as far as this logical progression can identify, the One True God, the creator God of the Bible, He who since the very beginning has been supporting every truth that has ever existed and ever will exist. He is the certain foundation upon which my Christian faith is built: God, the One and Only Certainty, He who calls Himself (*a statement of certainty*) 'I Am that I Am', as God referred to Himself while talking to Moses on Mount Sinai.

Here this chapter has reached its stated purpose of getting to the core of logic in order to identify the one underlying truth that supports all other truths. I suppose that is the proper place to end this chapter if I were merely looking to be scored well academically by my college professor. However, I'm no longer a starving college student, and my philosophy professor likely retired some years ago. Therefore, I'll disregard academic scoring of this chapter so that I may continue to move this chapter along.

Some people who have read this far into this chapter are overly sceptical; therefore, the only sense of certainty that they have gained from this chapter is the sense of certainty that my work in

National Expectations

this chapter has been wrong, sloppy, or just plain threatening to their sceptical sensibilities.

While overly sceptical people may think those things, overly certain people have perhaps found this chapter to be the sort of written ammunition that they find useful for shoving certainty down other people's throats.

Both of those sorts of readers have got what they wanted from this chapter, which is just more of the same sort of scepticism or certainty with which they came into this chapter.

Between those two extremes rest most people. One of the extreme sides consists of fundamentalists who doubt nothing that they believe. The opposite extreme side is extremely sceptical people who don't believe anything that can be doubted. These two extremes are opposites – two different sorts of literalism, two rigidities, two immovable extremes between which we reasonable people are somewhat stuck.

If, like me, you are reasonable, you are neither overly certain nor overly sceptical. If you are like me, then you and I share a common understanding that neither of us has everything worked out perfectly. If you are an imperfect person like me, then what I'm about to tell you about this chapter's topic is something you already know – that no human being needs to choose certainty or uncertainty.

We're human beings, not computers. Strict logic can't own you or me; nor can it ask us for a commitment. Strict logic can't do that to you, me, or any other human being because no human being is strictly logical. We humans weren't cut out to play logic's strict game; nor were we cut out to ignore logic altogether. We were cut out for something between those two extremes.

Between those two extremes are two things that break the laws of logic without breaking logic or breaking us humans. Those two things are humility and mercy. In short, aside from the two sorts of people who have already got what they wanted from this chapter, the rest of us have been cut out for humility and mercy. In more familiar terms, dear reader, we've been cut out to be Christians.

11
The Gift

Dear reader, the world is full of imperfect people who imperfectly write, imperfectly love, imperfectly speak, and imperfectly draw conclusions.

Considering that God knows all (He is omniscient), I'm not surprised that He gives mankind a gift for us to use to smooth out the rough, imperfect edges of ourselves, the rough, imperfect edges of each other, and the rough, imperfect edges of our societies.

People have always had various ideas about how they want to go about addressing mankind's imperfections. Therefore, the Gift has often been ignored in lieu of people's own imaginative ideas about how to deal with human imperfections.

As for me, however, when I'm faced with imperfections or limitations, I often simply reach for the Gift. It's a gift that when rejected can start wars, and when accepted can bring peace. It's a gift that when rejected can leave wounds opened, and when accepted, heals. It is, in my opinion, a divine gift that bridges the gaps between our imperfections and the higher hopes that God has for us. It's a divine gift that also bridges the gaps between our personal aspirations and true reality. This gift quiets arguments, stills waves, and rights the imperfectly innocent. It's a gift that a person can know they have accepted perhaps only when they show the Gift to other people.

The Gift is Mercy.

I know of that gift as well as I do only because of God's earlier gift, Jesus Christ.

12
Identity

In our present time (the 2020s), there is a peculiar identity problem in some of the nations of the Western world. This problem largely emerged with the drug-abusing hippie generation of the 1960s.

That problem of drug abuse, which marched in step with anonymous, meaningless sex and hostility towards most existing social norms, dropped its 'hippie' name in the 1970s in order to take on a more appealing name: being 'cool'. Then that 'cool' fraction of society became a new subculture. People in that subculture began thinking that being different was 'cool', and to not be different was 'uncool' and, counterintuitively, unpopular.

The 'cool' subculture continued to grow until the 1980s, when the AIDS epidemic and the US government's War on Drugs caused many 'cool' people in the US to reject drug abuse and promiscuous sex. That left alive only one aspect of their 'cool' subculture – hostility towards most social norms.

That hostility towards social norms necessitated that 'cool' people be originals unto themselves in ways that were obvious to other people. The peculiar result was that the requirement of *obvious* originality (individual difference) prohibited the psychological benefit of having a sense of belonging, because logically a person can't be *obviously* different from everyone else while simultaneously identifying with any group. As a result of this awkward situation that pop culture jumped towards several decades ago, many Americans and other Westerners developed a personal identity crisis that they're unaware of because it has been ingrained into some Western cultures.

National Expectations

During the 1990s, even though the 'cool' subculture did nothing to instil in people a sense of belonging, it became popular and therefore the cultural standard by which many people in society measured themselves and others. That raising of originality to a new cultural standard resulted in yet another problem.

Because the value of one's own originality is a difficult thing to measure or display to other people, these rebellious youths (*many of whom are now seniors with great-grandchildren*) began measuring themselves and other people by the most non-judgemental (*amoral*) things they could find: money and power.

When a person's primary focus is money and power, this is called materialism. These amoral 'cool' people are now greedy for money, power, or the combination of the two: social justice. However, psychologically, those people are seeking to be valued within the rest of the group of 'cool' amoral people. I suppose that some of them feel a minuscule sense of belonging within that amoral materialistic group of people, yet they have become as amoral as a pound coin. They're lost.

One important thing to note in this chapter's examination of *identity at work in a society* is that society didn't slip into materialism due to monetary greed, nor over-industrialization or economic pressures. Instead, Western society slipped into materialism when people who wanted to fit in with Western pop culture lost their identity. In turn, they then lost their healthy sense of belonging that's so important to mental health.

Now, because this chapter has contained subtle references to the relationship between self-identity (individualism) and group-identity (collectivism) or capital 'u' Unity, I think I'm obligated to have this book's next few chapters say a few words about unity, group communication, and collectivism.

13
A Certain Opinion

Certainty is a horrible place to begin writing a chapter partly because it ruins the suspense for the reader, and also partly because most conversations don't begin with a certainty (or rather a statement of certainty) and then converse forth in search of information that only supports the certainty with which the conversation began.

Most conversations don't proceed that backwards way; however, some modern conversations do, and some people's thought processes also work that backwards way because they want what they want regardless of whether what they want is right or wrong or makes good sense.

When socio-politically active people say to the people of their country, 'We need to have a conversation [about this or that issue],' reasonable people should expect a well-informed conversation, an intelligent conversation, or at least an open-minded conversation, rather than what passes for conversation in today's hyperactive socio-political Western world.

An obvious thing that we can assume about mankind's extremely ancient history is that prior to the development of human language, humans were unable to explain to one another why they were doing whatever they were doing. As long as they were doing good, and the people around them saw it as good, no explanation was really necessary. However, when an early human did a bad thing or something with which the other early humans disagreed, language allowed those early humans to expect explanations from one another. Of course, they didn't always get explanations. Or at least I'm fairly certain that was the case in prehistoric times, because I see something similar happening today regarding some very important socio-political issues. These issues are being talked about a lot, but not explained thoroughly at all.

Modern socio-political activists often say, 'We [referring to the people in their country] need to have a conversation,' but later when they carry on that conversation, they explain nothing. Instead, they state their opinions without offering a complete viewpoint which includes evidence that supports their reasoning and their reasoning's result – that result being their opinion.

Typical conversations are conversations of the friendly sort. Typical conversations don't require explanations to be articulated by the people who are conversing. However, when people say with seriousness to their fellow countrymen, 'We need to have a conversation [about this or that issue],' the suggestion is that during that conversation someone is going to explain themselves or the issue.

Conversations are not explanations, yet explanations are what socio-political people ask for when they say, 'We need to have a conversation.' And in a Western world that's currently full of conversations with few full explanations being articulated, the Age of Reason has become the Age of Excuses.

Some socio-political speakers in modern times can speak for an hour without saying anything substantive. They might as well simply walk to the microphone at their 'Social Justice' rally (or whatever), look sincerely towards the crowd, perhaps make eye contact with some members of the crowd in order to make a personal connection with their audience, and then say into the microphone, 'Ugh,' and be done with it.

The crowds at those rallies know what they want. The speakers know what they want. Many of the journalists who cover those rallies know what they want. Therefore, 'ugh' is really all that needs to be said by those individuals because almost no one goes to those energized rallies with an open mind. That's why I understand socio-political rallies (or socio-political YouTube videos) to be where people go mostly to dig deeper trenches and not to dig their way out of trenches.

National Expectations

All that's asked of the people who attend those sorts of rallies (or people massed together on social media) is that each person do nothing but believe what they already believe, think as they already think, or don't think as they already don't think.

Like those people whom I've just mentioned, I too appreciate people who agree with me. But, I also appreciate people who disagree with me. Perhaps that's selfish of me considering that I appreciate them because I've never been enlightened by someone with whom I already agree.

In past centuries, a great deal of thought went into creating the governments that exist in the Western world today. Yet now, after hundreds of years of each generation accepting their government's founding ideas as if those ideas were axioms that should be accepted without thought, many people have become somewhat thoughtless. Some people believe (like a constant religious experience) that their principles, or particular social justice cause, or their conservative theories, or progressive ideologies, are right and noble simply because people say those things are right and noble. There are lots of historically significant books of the political philosophy that influenced the founders of modern democracies and republics. Even today, those old historically significant books still support the wonderings and warnings of modern democratic and republican governments' founding ideas. However, the majority of people living today in those countries haven't read those founding books; nor do they intend to. Therefore, many Westerners today appear to be content to live within the constant religious experience of accepting people's word on many extremely important matters.

I didn't write the previous paragraph in order to weaken any democratic or republican government's founding ideas, but merely to point to the fact that some Western voters' brains have become lethargic.

In previous centuries people wanted self-government, then they put a lot of thought into justifying their self-governing bodies. Then they established their governments and subsequently napped for generations only to wake up to say, 'Democracy good. Kings bad. Ugh, ugh.' Then they congratulated one another for articulating their shared patriotism.

The Western world's democratic countries have very many founders from centuries past. The portion of those founders who didn't adopt other people's ideas merely for personal political gain were people who thought things through (to a large extent), and they asked their people to think things through also.

Some of the current Western countries' governmental founders debated among themselves about the possible best form of government for their land. Then they debated with their neighbours about how to form a government; metaphorically, that's to say, they debated about how to 'plant a fruit tree' of sorts. Yet, once you debate about the various ways of planting a fruit tree, eventually you either win the debate or you get won over by other people's ideas about how to plant that fruit tree, then you plant it, and that's followed by your children enjoying its fruit. Over time, the reasons why the fruit tree was planted that way are reasons that become lost to the shallow avarice of conspicuous consumption of one's ancestral fruit tree.

You would condemn a royal for doing such a thing; yet The People now do it and are pleased to call one another patriots. 'It's my country, and I can disrespect it all I want to,' they'll say in actions rather than words. But one word comes to my mind about all of this. That word is 'thoughtless'.

When your schools teach students what to think instead of how to think, some (but not all) students' reasoning capabilities are not as engaged as they'd otherwise be. That's when human desires (animalistic or otherwise) can be mistaken for facts. For thoughtless people, a simple one-line claim ought to be accepted by everyone as being a complete viewpoint. But, of course, a complete viewpoint includes evidence, logic, and sometimes statements of overt faith, not

National Expectations

covert faith. Complete viewpoints actually require more than a simple slogan or one-line claim.

The most that a one-line claim can be is a summary statement of a complete viewpoint. The worst a one-line claim can be is a lie.

Some socio-politically active people's thought-processes (at least their thought-processes they care to express publicly) begin with a stated claim (a conclusion), and then that person (*or even an entire 'Social Justice' movement*) doesn't even attempt to support their conclusion with legitimate evidence. For instance, when discussing the issue of elective abortion (non-medically necessary abortion), some people say, 'It's a Woman's Right to Choose [to kill her baby],' and they don't back up their claim with any good reasoning. Instead, they merely state their claim, and then they act as if their claim is a 'self-evident truth'.

I don't take issue with self-evident truths in general. In fact, I'll probably write in this book some claims that may appear as if I'm presenting them as self-evident truths, simply because I haven't described enough supporting evidence. If I do that in this book, it will open the door to my being seen as a hypocrite. But I assure you that hypocrisy is not evidence pertaining to any ideas or issues such as the issue of elective abortion. Instead, hypocrisy is only evidence of one's being a hypocrite. For instance, if the Pope had a girlfriend whom he impregnated, and then he asked his girlfriend to kill his child in the womb, that hypothetical situation wouldn't be evidence of elective abortions being moral and pleasing in God's eyes. Instead, that hypothetical situation would only be evidence that this hypothetical Pope was being a hypocrite several times over.

Likewise, if Gandhi had ever been poked in the eye by someone, and then he returned his injury by poking that person in the eye in retaliation, that hypothetical situation would make that hypothetical Gandhi a hypocrite. It would also point to his being human, like me, the person who's now writing this book, and like you, the person who's now reading it.

National Expectations

Even a blind squirrel occasionally finds a nut. Even a hypocrite can occasionally speak a truth. Even an imperfect human being like me can accurately point out that some people in modern times don't merely have backwards thought-processes: they actually seem to be lacking any thought-process at all. What I've observed is that some people begin their public comments by making a statement (a conclusion), and then they stop right there as if they had just stated a self-evident truth, an axiom, a certainty.

Some amount of certainty is a wonderful place to begin or renew a nation because it can anchor a nation. However, certainty is a horrible place to start a thought-process, a book, or a conversation such as this one in which I now ask you to consider what passes for a self-evident truth these days.

I'll here begin our considerations of self-evident truths by examining some obvious things about basic mathematics' self-evident truths.

National Expectations

Contrary to popular notions, 2 + 2 = 4 is not actually a self-evident truth unless you know in advance how the mathematics of addition work. You have to work through it and have some knowledge before you can rightly consider anything to be a self-evident truth. A three-year-old child wouldn't consider 2 + 2 = 4 as being a self-evident truth until after that child understood what the '+' sign meant or what the words 'plus' or 'add' mean.

'The Sun will rise tomorrow morning' is a statement that is extremely believable, but it can't be a self-evident truth until tomorrow morning. The sunny point here is that sometimes patience is required before evidence exists that either proves or disproves a presumably self-evident truth.

So now, when people say, 'It's a woman's right to choose [to kill her child in the womb],' where's the evidence of that statement being true? I'm not asking whether you or anyone thinks it's morally right or wrong. Instead, I'm asking for the evidence that supports the deadly statement.

National Expectations

Where's the evidence that supports the statement, 'It's a woman's right to choose [to kill human life in the womb]'?

If a person proves beyond a reasonable doubt that 'inconvenience' is a crime punishable by death, then that proof would of course have to consist of solid evidence supporting the notion that murdering 'inconvenient' human beings is the right thing to do inside or outside the womb. However, that question about murdering 'inconvenient' human beings isn't a valid question because no human being's convenience or inconvenience can be completely measured by anyone. Here I'll leave that statement as a self-evident truth simply so that some readers can chew on it if they'd like to.

How about the question of unwanted human life? I safely assume that wanted babies are not the human beings who are losing their lives in abortion clinics. Therefore, just for a moment we should focus our mindfulness towards those of us who are most applicable to this consideration: unwanted human beings.

National Expectations

The term 'unwanted' is a difficult term to define when life-and-death questions require a great degree of accuracy. Therefore, let's not endlessly split hairs here, but instead ask ourselves the next question in this line of enquiry. That question is, 'Is one's situation of being "unwanted" a crime punishable by death [in the womb]?'

If one believes and claims that one's being 'unwanted' is something they or any other human being should be killed for or murdered for, and that person had verifiable evidence to support their deadly claim, then the question is, 'Is the evidence they have enough to prove their deadly claim beyond a reasonable doubt?'

If a person believes that the people in their country (people under their communal rule in a democratic country) ought to be allowed to legally kill the Unwanted, then we have to ask the question 'Is any human being entirely unwanted?'

Underneath that question is a string of philosophical questions and answers that few

National Expectations

people care to read, and that usually end with a question some people (but not I) seem to enjoy asking. That question is, 'Does life have purpose?'

If human life has no purpose, then logic dictates that the yet-born child has no purpose, nor does his or her mother and father. That points to an abysmal equality for all human beings, but it's equality all the same.

I just so happen to think that life is a blessing and that we're all equally blessed by receiving one life each. Other people just so happen to think that life is hell, and that we're all equally cursed by receiving one life each. Who's in the light and who's in the dark on that specific issue doesn't matter to the point here, because regardless of the various ways people define equality, there is only one overarching concept of equality, and that concept pertains to the Living rather than the Dead. Therefore, even if you think that life has no purpose, even if you believe that human life is a curse, even if you believe that there is no meaning in life, even then you and I'd probably agree that the living and the dead are not equals, yet living human beings are equals.

Human life in the womb is not dead. Therefore, human life in the womb and human life outside the womb are equals. That's a logical conclusion which is more than self-evident because I just described that conclusion's supportive reasoning.

Regarding self-evident truths, it's worth my repeating a couple things I've written for you earlier

2 + 2 = 4 is not actually a self-evident truth unless you know in advance how the mathematics of addition work. Similarly, 'The Sun will rise tomorrow morning' is a statement that is extremely believable, but it can't be a self-evident truth until tomorrow morning. The sunny point there is that sometimes patience is required before evidence exists that either proves or disproves a presumably self-evident truth.

Now, nearing the end of this chapter, and prepared with thoughtfulness and patience enough to see one's way through to a well-reasoned answer, I ask people on both sides of the argument, when people say, 'It's a woman's right to choose [to kill her child in the womb],' where's the evidence that proves that deadly statement is true beyond a reasonable doubt?

If a person has only an opinion with no complete answer or evidence, yet that person supports the killings anyway, then it stands to reason that that person supports the killings or murders, not by way of good reasoning on their part, but instead by way of their faith; for what is believed without reason can only be believed by faith.

Therefore, it stands to reason that my opponents on this issue support the killing or murdering of innocent human beings as a matter of their faith. That statement is not my mere opinion; instead, it's a valid statement I've spent much of this chapter substantiating.

Unsubstantiated opinions, as popular and powerful as they are in today's Western countries, have, on this particular life and death issue, turned the Age of Reason into the Age of Excuses, turned morality into a statistical derivative, turned humanity into a question of convenience, turned courts against the innocent, extinguished the thoughtful 'Age of Enlightenment' for the sake of a thoughtless 'Age of Dim', and mistaken the Living for the Dead.

14

Words, Progress, and People

It used to be the case that when someone misused a word, it was simply called a mistake because it was usually accidental. In those older days, intentional misuse of words was confined mostly to sarcastic remarks, which were usually obvious and never intended to be taken literally. However, over the last few decades, intentionally deceptive misuse of words (which is something that liars do) has been repackaged and come to be popularly referred to as 'politically correct speech' or 'PC'.

After 'politically correct' speech took root in pockets of Western society, some people began stringing 'politically correct' words together in order to form sentences containing intentionally deceitful ideas. Those deceitful ideas have now come to be referred to by some people as 'alternative facts', which is the 'politically correct' phrase for a lie.

I can't read those nonsensical 'PC' people's hearts and minds in order to know their deepest motivations for their inaccurate word usage. Nonetheless, from a psychological perspective, it appears that they twist words for two general reasons. One obvious reason is that today's Western societies are mostly democratic, meaning that the majority population – mathematically guided by popular ideals measured by ballot boxes and opinion polls – holds ultimate power over everyone. Therefore some people find it to be a benefit for them to fit in with whatever ideals are perceived to be popular, to reject ideals that are perceived to be unpopular, and to attempt to survive safely as an individual person in the communal system of democratic society. So, sometimes a person's twisting of words is the result of their just trying to fit in with the majority of people. Those people have no nefarious intentions or ill will. They're just trying to survive as best as they can.

Aside from twisting words in order to safely survive by fitting in, there are other reasons why some people twist words. In modern times, there are still some people twisting words for the ancient reason of arrogance. Arrogance in as much the twisting of words always avails the opportunity for a user of 'politically correct' speech to attempt to publicly establish the seemingly undeniable fact that they're a person who's 'other than the past', a social innovator, and a person who's politically relevant because they're in possession of intelligence so mighty that they can forge a better future for mankind by merely changing the connotations or definitions of existing words; for instance, changing the word 'mankind' to 'humanity'.

If a hog could talk, he'd tell you that he doesn't taste delicious. He'd tell you this because he doesn't want you to think that he tastes delicious; but, honestly, he really hasn't a clue. So too, if an

National Expectations

unscrupulous idiot could talk (and they do so more than most people), they'd tell you that their words are true and that their scruples are above reproach. Regardless of the particular motivations that each liar might have for twisting words into politically pleasing music to the democratic ear ('politically correct' speech), and regardless of what is in their heart or what is shoved into their heads, what comes out of their mouths are lies.

Misinformation is not a modern invention. Misinformation was pointed out to human beings by highlighting it in history dating back to the Garden of Eden. For you readers who are non-Christians who reject the Bible (and therefore completely reject the story in the Garden of Eden), I tell you with nearly absolute certainty that the world has had liars in it ever since human beings realized that they couldn't read one another's minds.

It took thousands of years for mankind to climb up the hill away from early man's instinctual prehistoric selfishness in order for us to be safe from one another's deceptions. Mankind did that

National Expectations

partly by coming to value honesty in ourselves and in those around us. Yet, times have changed. It seems now that portions of mankind are attempting to progress beyond the virtue of honesty, and they have moved on to the fake virtue of 'progress' – as if all progress is inherently virtuous. It's not.

With increasing obviousness, it seems that the most vociferous Western people (a loud minority) believe that an honest life is not enough for them or other people. One of the reasons for this is that young people have been taught to believe that they're responsible for, in some grand fashion, 'Changing the World', or, as the humblest of arrogant people say, 'Make a Difference [in a large way]'.

Of course, honest lives automatically make a positive difference in the world. However, that honest positive difference is not enough for many supposedly 'modern' people.

Portions of Western society have moved away from honesty and moved towards 'progress' for

National Expectations

progress' sake. Therefore, now some of our people value things and people simply for their originality, regardless of the person's authenticity and genuine good character. Some people have been led to undervalue their own authenticity and honesty while they inaccurately measure their personal value in the manner that popular society informs them to measure all people – by 'newness'. Newness as far as their opinions and word choices can display to their friends and selected enemies.

One result of that 'progressive' nonsense and 'newspeak' is that people now often argue about words (mere labels for things) instead of addressing reality in a world in which, if you haven't enough food, you starve to death; if you haven't enough of the correct medicine, then you and your loved ones could die; and if you don't have healthy international relationships, then a foreign army could annihilate you and enslave your children. All of those long-existing realities are ignored while popular idiots argue about words. Today, if Western society were written into words, it would read like Douglas Adams's descriptions of George Orwell's nightmares.

Teenagers have a seemingly natural desire to moderately rebel as they approach adulthood and the responsibilities that accompany adulthood. It used to be that the list of adult responsibilities was a short list, which included important things such as one's responsibility to live an honest life and be respectful towards other people. Those are still on the short list that I'll be handing to my children. Yet modernity has placed upon many other Western teenagers the expectation that they're supposed to 'Change the World' or 'Make a Difference' in grand ways.

This socio-psychological deterioration has come partly from warped grandiose academic professors squeezing unnatural ambitions from our young people while pop culture and politicians' speeches paint unrealistic pictures of what can actually be achieved. Some adults teach our children that science, government policies, and pop culture's usefulness towards destroying existing systems that have been labelled as 'old' are what a good life is all about. They teach our children to destroy things. Some educators, some politicians, many media personalities, and even some parents, teach young people to rebel, destroy, hate, and seek vengeance – such as the forcing of white people to their knees as a sign of 'justice'.

Modern pop culture (including academia, news organizations, social media, and some popular public figures) in Western society teaches our children to be bad people. And as some Western societies do that cruel thing, teen suicide rates shoot through the roof, drug abuse sends many young people to their graves, mass shootings have become common in some Western countries, and sometimes frustrated mentally ill citizens drive their vehicles over pedestrians gathered on the streets and pavements as they protest something in order to 'Make a Difference in the World' in one way, while the frustrated mentally ill person in the vehicle seeks to 'Make a Difference in the World' in another way.

Over a long period of time, our Western society has institutionalized rebellion. The West has made rebellion a way of life. Mainstream Western society has taught our children that it's virtuous to knock down people and things. And in this unhealthy social environment that deceptive social leaders have made by twisting words for the sake of increased social relevancy or political gain, our children are killing themselves and others.

Words can wound. Words can heal. And the twisting of words can drive people and nations insane and create dystopian societies. That brings us to this book's next chapter, which is a useful response to George Orwell's novel *1984*.

National Expectations

15
1985: A Useful Response to George Orwell's novel 1984

In some ways this entire book is a response to collectivist dystopias the likes of which author George Orwell warned the public about. In my estimation, George Orwell's warnings in his book *1984* somewhat support Dr Carl Jung's concerns about a side of the human mind that Dr Jung called 'The Shadow'. Perhaps even more, *1984*'s psychological undercurrent seems to run parallel with some of Jean Baudrillard's observations of postmodernism at work in Western societies. Therefore, this chapter is not a response merely to one man's book (Orwell's *1984*); instead, this chapter's response is to many people's observations and subsequent concerns about the Western world's societies losing their grip on

National Expectations

reality, which is a step towards dystopias and other communal tragedies.

As a response that will hinder an Orwellian nightmare from manifesting itself in your society, I suggest here something fairly simple. I suggest particularly to other Christian parents that they inform their descendants about who they (we Christian parents) are as individual people rather than, after we're dead, leaving the earthly memories of ourselves to be defined by the biased brush strokes with which history books and news journalists tend to paint entire societies and historical groups of people.

I don't suppose that every descendant in the future will want to know their parent, grandparent, or other ancestors in any manner whatsoever. Nonetheless, as part of those children's rightful inheritance, Christian parents ought to make some information about themselves available (not necessarily publicly) to their descendants as part of their inheritance from our generation.

National Expectations

I make these suggestions to Christian parents rather than to non-Christian parents partly because most of the Western world's non-Christians are atheists who are moral relativists. Considering that moral relativism is, by definition, pertinent only to a particular time, place, and person, it would be antithetical to a moral relativist's sensibilities for him or her to even think of leaving anything of moral relevance to their descendants.

You see, dear reader, a moral relativist's own convictions suggest that their ideas regarding morality will be out of fashion soon after they're dead. Therefore, if I were to suggest here to a moral relativist (non-Christian) that their current convictions remained memorable or noteworthy after they were dead, I'd be insulting their most fundamental moral relativistic belief. Therefore, I can't make these same suggestions to moral relativist parents as I can to Christian parents.

Obviously, not every Christian parent needs to make their writing open to the general public as I'm doing with this book. However, even a short note written by you, addressed to your descendants, that reads, 'You don't belong to the World. You belong to me, and I belong to you, Jesus Christ, and God,' is really all that's needed to be left by you as an inheritance for your children to pass on to all of your descendants. This will serve to remind them that they, their brothers, sisters, and children don't belong to the world, that they're not the playthings of their governments or their neighbours, their property is not their neighbours' property, and that your descendants ought not to be the targets of dishonest rhetoric spewed out by socio-political activists, morally relativistic popularity brokers, dishonest news media personalities, and other activists who want to change the world by changing you and your children through collectivism, the power of the popular vote, unity for unity's sake, fear mongering, or other methods of binding people together for the supposed Greater (yet unattainable) Good.

When people devalue individual human freedom in order to overvalue socio-political

National Expectations

daydreams, then those people will be led to believe that personal freedom is not enough. They will then hunger for, and invent, an imagined 'Greater Good'. That's why we live in a time when our people's individual freedoms are traded across the legislative floors of Washington DC, Brussels, and elsewhere as if the freedoms granted by God to our children are pork bellies traded across the stock market floors of legislatures that are fuelled by the base currency of voters' and politicians' own popularity, the social security found in popularity, and popularity used as medication to treat one's own primal fears of standing alone with one's own integrity.

The list of side effects resulting from that medication of popularity are as follows: habitual compromise, loss of integrity, memory loss, confusion, poor judgment, and a step towards the dismantling of each person's genuine individual identity – a person's complete and unique personality, or what some people might consider basically to be a person's soul. Such is the meal served at the collectivists' banquet.

National Expectations

Dear Christian reader, please consider the Bible, remember the wars of the twentieth century and other senseless atrocities, consider the work of analytical psychology's founder Dr Jung concerning what he called 'The Shadow', consider Jean Baudrillard's observations regarding postmodernism's insanity. Of course, please also consider the more easily understood concerns of George Orwell regarding dystopias, consider what I've written in this book thus far, and consider the presently confused state of the world. Or just simply reflect on the Bible and then, dear Christian reader, please understand that if you don't claim your children, the World will.

I suggest to Christian parents that they claim their children not by telling their children who they are, but rather whose they are. To quote George Orwell from one of his last video-recorded interviews, 'The answer is you.'

16
National Treasure

While working through the challenge of writing this book from America for British readers, I necessarily had a unique vantage point from which to view the 'National Treasure' that, as one modern legend stated, was in 1776 too much 'treasure' for any one person to hold. As that legend portrays the treasure, it was hidden away by the socio-political experimenting founders of the Republic.

The real treasure which, in the 1700s and earlier, was thought to be too much for one man to hold, was metaphorically portrayed fairly recently in the Nicholas Cage film *National Treasure*. In that film the treasure was a massive amount of gold

National Expectations

and valuable ancient artefacts buried deep within the nation's soil.

However, the real treasure is not material. And the real soil of any nation is not its land so much as that nation's people. You see, when the experiments in democracy began, the trust that people had historically placed in their monarchs was taken and buried deep in the soil of the nation's people. It was shut away, locked behind a legal document, made the butt of jokes, ridiculed, literally beheaded in some countries, shot to death in other countries.

The real treasure, which the founding experimenters decided was too much for one man to be trusted with, is trust itself: the people's trust. Trust in a king, trust in a man as being an honest king of integrity, compassion, and wisdom, a person worth keeping, a domestic peace keeper and protector of the innocent, a steadfast standard, a guidepost, an advisor, a father.

A nation's profound treasure is the trust that helps to build families, communities, nations, tolerance, and humanity. For centuries now off the shores of Great Britain, such treasure has been buried in the soil of men and women, and generation after generation of people have suffered in its absence. In the absence of trust, fear breeds fear, distrust widens social divides, and eventually reason collapses along with that society. And that society stays down until they relearn that trust is national treasure.

National Expectations

National Expectations

17
The Future

When I consider the future, I'm as blind as a bat. However, I become a little less blind when I consider something that Jesus said regarding the future. I'm referring specifically to Jesus' statement 'Blessed are the meek, for they shall inherit the earth.'

People who are not meek are ambitious (obviously).

Some people are ambitious for money, which is a grudge against the condition of one's wallet or bank account. People who succumb to the ambition of being supremely intelligent have a grudge against their current intellectual abilities. People who have the grand ambition to change the world in grand ways apparently have a grudge against the world as the world is.

National Expectations

Today's Western world has many ambitious people and few meek people. Today's Western world has many people who carry various sorts of grudges, and too few people who set down grudges in order to accept the world as it is.

One of the things I have to say here about the future is something that concerns your future inheritance. It really concerns everyone's future inheritance, but mostly the meek people's inheritance of the earth.

Far be it from me to suggest to you that I know what Jesus actually meant when He made His famous statement while He delivered His Sermon on the Mount. But considering that non-meek people reject the earth as it is, perhaps, just perhaps, the meek shall inherit the earth because they're the only human beings who will ever accept it.

18
The Great Negotiation

There are currently some discussions being had in Ireland about a referendum to legally unite the island of Ireland under one Irish government. I won't discuss the politics of that referendum. Even if I did want to say something political about it, I'd be wasting words because most people in the voting population have already made up their minds. Therefore, there isn't a great deal of negotiating going on inside individual people's minds as to which way they will vote.

So, instead of commenting on those negotiations, I'll comment on a negotiation that is more fundamental. It's the great negotiation between complexity and simplicity.

Complexity is commonly produced as the natural result of people surrendering to the fact

National Expectations

that life isn't as simple as they first thought it was. Other times, complexity increases when we get ourselves involved in legal issues, such as international agreements. Such agreements are beneficial if not entirely necessary. Therefore, I must admit that some complexity is unavoidable.

However, sometimes complexity is produced needlessly when some people try proving to you how intelligent they are, or when people tell you exactly how things ought to be even though they haven't a clue. There are not many ways to make or keep things simple. However, there are virtually a limitless number of ways for people to make things more complicated than those things need to be.

As far as the referendum regarding Northern Ireland, I don't think that there is, in this entire world, enough complex legal gobbledegook, or complex history, or complicatedly worded ballot referendums to do Ireland's people more good than can simplicity.

National Expectations

You see, dear reader, before people became forced to do the complex work of deciding what flag to follow, they were freer. And before nationhood was made complex, it was simple.

That is the subject of this book's next chapter.

National Expectations

19
National Fidelity (a poem)

Before the nations of the Western world followed popular opinions and so became 'ideas' (for instance, many Americans say, 'America is an idea,' and many Europeans say, 'The European Union is an idea'), the nations of the Western world were not notions; instead, we were nations.

Nations have borders, whereas notions do not.

Nations have laws, whereas notions merely have debatable arguments.

Nations can keep their noses out of other people's business, whereas notions lack such good neighbourliness.

Nations are solid, whereas notions ooze.

National Expectations

Nations are safe havens for their people, whereas notions look for their own safe haven in your mind.

Before the nations of the Western world began bequeathing to their children notions (ideas to spread, die for, and kill for), our ancestors bequeathed to their children nations: homelands, law, tradition, history, wisdom, character, integrity, and security. Before we trusted the common stranger, we trusted our loved ones.

Before blood-drenched notions forced us to understand that the pen is mightier than the sword, we understood that neither was required where there was compassion.

Before politics spurred us to think as a Left or Right collective, we were free to think for ourselves.

Before we loved flags, we loved one another – and we were nations.

Before we were proud, we were grateful.

National Expectations

Before we operated the State and so the State operated us, you didn't try to operate me; well, not so much.

Before we admired political manoeuvres, we admired honesty and honest people.

Before radicals began taking advantage of us by 'never letting a crisis go to waste', we helped one another work around crisis.

Before we 'Built Back Better for ourselves', we built trust among ourselves.

Before we progressed towards moulding one another into globally pleasing citizens of sameness, we were each extraordinary – and we were nations.

The Western world comes from ancestors who, although not perfect, did aspire to lead honest lives in which they said what they would do and they did what they said. But now under intrusive communal rule and led by tumultuous societies, we say what our neighbours should do, and we do what our neighbours say.

National Expectations

Before we conserved legal precedent, we conserved life – and we were nations.

Before we served notions, we served our children – and we were trusted.

Before we were guilty, we were innocent.

And before it all, we were home, loved by our loved ones – and we were nations.

20
My British Ancestor's Eyes

My fabled ancestor's position as 'The First Among Equals' was the result of timing. The word 'first' in the phrase 'The First Among Equals' comes from chronology (timing), and it doesn't refer to his winning first place in a fencing competition or popularity contest.

Go back thousands of years prior to my fifth-century ancestor's life, and you will reach our earliest known paternal biological ancestor and his wife who were the very first couple whose descendants were Iceni and eventually amalgamated into the Britons of today.

That very first Iceni or British man's firstborn son was literally the first among his generation.

National Expectations

The generation that followed that generation also had a firstborn. And although everyone in each generation was equal, there was continually only one 'first'. Of course, as time went by the family grew, and all the while there continued to be only one 'First Among Equals'.

In the position of being 'The First Among Equals', it was his job to make final decisions in his courtroom after hearing from everyone else – all of whom were his equal and one another's equals as well. That system of chronology combined with mutual respect is where the references to the legendary 'The First Among Equals' comes from.

By coming into office by unbiased means (those means being tamper-proof chronology), his world view would likely have been more unbiased than most people's world views simply for the fact that . . . Well, let me put it to you this way – if everyone tells you that you were born into victimhood, you are likely to be biased towards looking for victims and victimizers. Similarly, if people tell you that you were born into an unjust economic system that separates people into groups of rich and poor, then you are likely going to become biased towards seeing people as being either rich or poor, and perhaps too much of either one.

When a person is born into a position decided by the calendar every generation going back as far as your history can take you, that is as unbiased a way as is possible to determine who's literally first.

The judiciously beneficial product of being positioned as the result of unbiased natural things (such as a calendar's passing of days) is that you will be more likely to be biased towards being unbiased. Yes, I'm aware that that sounds odd; nonetheless, it's correct to say 'biased towards being unbiased'. Perhaps that will sound less odd after you read the next few paragraphs.

Very likely no one can remove all biases from themselves or anyone else. One reason for that is that the human mind organizes information into a structure of priorities, categories, classifications, and such. It's necessary for the human mind to

National Expectations

organize information in that way because otherwise the information isn't organized in any way whatsoever. Stark raving lunatics' minds have no organization of their thoughts and incoming information. However, mentally healthy people's minds do organize thoughts and incoming information. That organization requires structure, and that structure of information is what results in the person being biased. Therefore, we have to conclude that all (or nearly all) mentally healthy people are somewhat biased in their decision-making processes.

The best that anyone can do to mitigate inherent biases is not to attempt the impossible wiping away every bias, but instead to bias towards non-bias. That's exactly what the positioning as 'first' does. That tradition is still carried on in the British monarchy today.

In modern times, many people frown on the institution of monarchy because the monarchical system isn't easy to tamper with - And people very much enjoy tampering with things and one another. Yet, if you or any other modern person were alive when my AD 432 ancestor was positioned as 'The First Among Equals', you probably would have seen his leading position of 'First' being as fair as a clock, as unbiased as a calendar, and as useful as a compass that always points our people home.

If you were alive during the first half of the first millennium AD, then you probably would have seen the situation as it truly is – natural.

And although my fabled ancestor might not have heard of the term 'Natural Law' in his court, his court operated under Natural Law.

That is the subject of this book's next chapter.

National Expectations

21
Natural Law

If a person were to attempt to define exactly what Natural Law is that person would be acting as unrealistically as a tree that tried to feed itself on mice, or a cat that sprawled in the sunshine in an insane attempt to feed itself by way of photosynthesis.

That insane cat would starve to death, and although that crazy tree wouldn't be able to stop growing, it would become quite upset by never being able to taste a mouse. So too, some humans (political philosophers mostly) have driven themselves and other people bonkers by trying to define exactly what Natural Law is.

People are not able to identify Natural Law as well as people are able to identify un-natural law. The justifiable reason for this is that God defines what nature (including Natural Law) is. We human beings can't define Natural Law due to the fact that we're a product of nature. By definition, all that we humans do is artificial, and because we can identify artificial things, we can clear away those artificial things (corruption, biases and such) so that we don't corrupt our understanding of Natural Law.

In that sense, Natural Law is what we might see of law if we humans never put a finger on it.

I can draw an analogy by mentioning that in the science of physics, the first law of motion is that a body at rest tends to remain at rest until acted upon by an outside force. Dear reader, we humans are the analogous 'outside force' that can put Natural Law out of rest, thereby removing it from its natural state and causing our perceptions of it to become skewed by our own clumsy ignorant human desires, biases, goals, and such.

So, if you want to understand Natural Law, then get your hands off it, back away, get a glimpse of it from a distance, and understand that authentic Natural Law is off limits to us human beings. Nonetheless, we humans can identify the artificial things such as biases, goals, and corruptions, which we ought not to allow to act upon our society's legal decisions.

People's understanding of authentic Natural Law as being 'beyond human view' and understanding that artificial things (biases and such) are not beyond human view are the two basic ingredients of the legal systems of the Western world of today.

Those two ingredients are what have led some modern 'Progressive' people to perceive their nations' Written Constitutions as a list of 'Negative Rights' – a list of things that the People and their government can't do.

Well, dear reader, you wouldn't be very free if you lived under a written constitution that told you what you must do daily in great detail. Therefore, I hope that you appreciate living with a government that, for the most part, tells you and government employees what you and they must not do.

I'll now mention a simple legal concept that may put the majority of this book into perspective for you. I can explain this simple concept to the broader audience most easily with another analogy here. Now, if you walked into a courtroom in London and asked a judge to convince you that their ruling in a particular case was right and just, you would be upside down because it has never been any judge's job to convince anyone about any court decision. Judges are not in the role of convincing other people. Instead, judges are in the role of being convinced by evidence and oral arguments put to them by attorneys on two or more sides of a court case.

Judges are not in the role of convincing other people. Therefore, I think that you can understand that this book's attention given to the Saint Patrick-inspired fifth century court case about Christianity and British society was never intended to convince any reader of anything other than how very convinced the author (me) is that our society's adoption of the Holy Bible and our society's embracing of Christianity has been, and continues to be, good for our society.

With that now said here near the end of this book, dear reader, you and I have arrived back to the main point that I made in chapter two's poem 'The Rugged Road of Freedom', when I wrote, *I cannot prove all of the good things which I believe; yet, I am free to prove that I believe them.* So are you dear Western reader.

Now that this book has circled back to the topic of 'proof' just after discussing natural law and describing some fundamentals of court proceedings, I consider this chapter to be the last chapter you can accept as court submittals pertaining to the AD432 case regarding Christianity and British society.

With all of that due diligence sufficiently exercised thus far in this book, it is time 'go to court' in this book's next and last chapters, which are The Crown's Court Opinion (AD432) and The Defunct Crown's Court Opinion (AD2025).

National Expectations

22
The Crown's Court Opinion (AD 432)

The historical events depicted in this chapter are events which also occurred millions of times over while Christianity spread through Europe and other parts of the world. Therefore, dear reader, at least one or two of your ancestors were, at some point in history, placed in a situation to hear about Christianity and Jesus for the first time, and then form some opinion about it. Those particular ancestors of yours are little different from the one depicted in this chapter.

Because the historical event depicted in this chapter occurred when the court was hearing about Christianity for the first time, I've written this court's opinion with very few if any theological points *included. It was honest of me to write it in that manner. However, it will make this AD 432 court's opinion feel dry and bland to readers. But I assure you that the adjectives 'dry' and 'bland' have always been part and parcel of pragmatic people and courts who hear national security matters that require pragmatism for everyone's sake.*

British Society with Christianity

vs.

British Society without Christianity

The Crown's Court Opinion

The court has reviewed the Holy Bible in comparison to our people's recorded history and has noticed an irreconcilable discrepancy in the two timeframes, but also many remarkable similarities between the two histories.

The court finds the New Testament and Christianity to be consistent with our people's efforts to maintain clear lines between literal and non-literal information, timely details and timeless lessons, slavery of the human mind under a theocracy as opposed to the freedom found by each of our people when they are left to reason for themselves.

Theology aside, this court sees that Jesus' life lived as the Son of God posed a non-theological question that most of the people of the biblical lands did not want to answer, and therefore they seem to have never bothered to ask themselves. The question that Jesus' life put to biblical literalists of his day was this: 'So, Jesus had a biological father, yet Adam and Eve did not?' That is the question which perhaps spurred Jesus to say that no one comes to the father except through Him. Knowing what I know about our ancient history's timescale, it seems to this court that Jesus' statement was not arrogant, but instead it was realistic, likely based in biology, was counter-zealot (counter-extremist), and had a great deal to do with Jesus' freeing people from their deadly pursuit of unattainable literal perfection of one another in their theocratic society.

The statements Jesus made, and the humble question His life put to the people of the biblical lands, required from Jesus an immeasurable amount of self-sacrifice given to His people in His efforts to save them from the collective literalism of religious laws that led to some people being stoned to death or being gravely injured due to the public's religious zeal and extreme fundamentalism.

Jesus' life and his question helped some of His people to awaken from the collective delusion that God would only accept them after their perfection by law.

In the light of those realistic assertions I have just noted, this court finds Christianity and *the New Testament* to be so correct, good, and irreplaceable that I have become a Christian myself. However, the Old Testament's timeframe causes my role as 'The

National Expectations

First Among Equals' to be drawn into question by literal interpretations of the Old Testament's Jewish timeframe.

We know that the Old Testament's timeframe is inaccurate, yet today (approximately AD 432) we have no tangible evidence that indicates our non-Jewish timeframe is accurate.

Our people cannot be asked to live with two conflicting literal timeframes, one being our Celtic timeframe and the other timeframe being that of the Jewish people as described in the Old Testament and professed by the Roman Empire today. Obviously, someone's timeframe is wrong; therefore, I would rule against this new religion simply due to Rome's stance. However, Christianity is too important for me to allow Rome's adoption of Jewish details risk our people missing out on Christianity.

Christianity is important for many reasons, not the least of which is that the world is either saved by a universal love story, or the world is not saved at all. Love stories are selfless. Selfless thoughts are those that have us put ourselves aside so that we can think

National Expectations

without our biases, prejudices, and self-centredness getting in the way of our clearer reasoning and kindness shown to our neighbours. Selfless thoughts are required if we are ever to live in a just world; when people can often turn to one another for just treatment instead of always needing to come to local courts or my court for justice. Love stories urge us to subdue our fears and to think straight. And only a universal love story can have that good effect beyond the borders of the British Isles.

We do not get to pick and choose which universal love story came first. We know that that first universal love story was The Life and Passion of Jesus Christ. He was the first. There is no replacement. Therefore, The Life and Passion of Jesus Christ was the first universal love story as well as the last. I am the 'The First Among Equals' who must bow to Jesus who has no equal. He was the first and the last (the Alpha and Omega) as well as the King of kings.

Jesus is irreplaceable for more reasons than I could ever hope to understand. Yet, I can easily point out the obvious – that he is irreplaceable due to the

National Expectations

fact that anyone who ignores Jesus' universal love story in order to play out a different universal love story would be acting selfishly, and therefore removing the selflessness required of a universal love story capable of saving the world from itself.

Tradition obligates me to explain my decision so that our people can understand my court's decision. Yet because of our present circumstances I cannot have my reasoning made public. Therefore, today I am left with no better option than to quietly put down my crown until such time that evidence appears as to whether our Celtic timeline or the Jewish timeline is more correct. When that discrepancy in the two timelines is resolved, then perhaps one of my heirs can write my opinion in a book that can give our future generations an understanding of why I ruled in favour of Christianity and why I had to rest my crown for our people's sake.

Until that discrepancy in the timelines is resolved and one of my descendants writes my opinion in a book, our future generations can refer to

National Expectations

him and me together simply as our people's Once and Future King.

Summary: In the case of British society with Christianity vs. British society without Christianity, This court rules in favour of British society with Christianity.

<u>*King Prasutagus XIX*</u>

The Crown's signature

23

The Defunct Crown's Court Opinion (AD 2025)

British Society with Christianity

vs.

British Society without Christianity

The court (retired, questionable, and defunct as it is in AD2025) has reviewed the Holy Bible, Christianity, biology, sociology, psychology, political philosophy, ethics, moral philosophy, natural law, history, the relationship between law and mercy, and human beings' habitual dystopian pursuit of perfection.

The court believes that the 1593 years of additional human experience and Western intellectual development that have taken place since AD 432 allow people today to better understand the differences between each other's cultures, and the differences between human beings and divine beings. Therefore, Jesus' divinity as described in John 3:16 ought to be less disputable today than it was in AD 432, when my predecessor avoided commenting on Jesus' divinity in his Written Court's Opinion. In both cases and times, Jesus' divinity remains an unprovable matter of faith, and a matter that has visibly sustained my own eternal hope and the eternal hope of countless other Britons over the past 1593 years. We can't separate what is sustained (eternal hope) from what sustains it (Jesus Christ).

After patiently reflecting on this information, and related documents, this court has formed and summarized its judgment as follows:

Summary: In the case of British society with Christianity vs. British society without Christianity, This court rules in favour of British society with Christianity.

National Expectations

Case Closed

The Defunct Crown's signature

Court exhibits attached – Chapters 2–22

End

National Expectations

Appendix A –
A Declaration of Interdependence

Independence and Interdependence are inextricably tied to the human experience as well as to the basic cause-and-effect relationships present throughout the universe.

Independence and interdependence complement one another. They are two sides of the same coin; both sides together giving depth, dimension and vitality to the whole.

It isn't always easy to level one's self with the other side of a closely-held ideology. Therefore, this writing for Britain 'A Declaration of Interdependence' will appear to be upside down to some people. However, it is right-side up for British people because within this declaration rests what I think may be Britain's reasoning for having the National Healthcare Service (NHS), as well as why Charles Dickens was unsurprisingly British, and why The British Commonwealth of Nations can be accurately described as a family.

A Declaration of Interdependence

*W*hen *in the course of human events, any one young human being becomes, for better or worse, separated from their biological parents and therefore left unnaturally independent, then for the sake of future generations it becomes necessary for that lone son or daughter to tether their self to a good fatherly and motherly example (adoptive parents) and to assume among the powers of the earth, the separate and equal station to which the Laws of Nature and of Nature's God entitle that child to ground themselves in parents of the good character that sustains wellbeing, familial duty, and the ineffable commonality of their British people.*

*W*e *hold these truths to be self-evident, that all men are created equal, that they are endowed by their Creator with certain unalienable Rights, that* among these are life and the right to the interdependence of family bonds.--That to secure these rights, mercy exists and laws of adoption are instituted among the British, deriving their just powers from the needs of children, --That whenever present circumstances become destructive of goodness, it is the Right and Duty of the son or daughter to abolish that deficiency by reconstituting goodness through lifelong attention given to good adoptive fatherly and motherly examples, and through familial efforts particular to the British, and with resolute trust in the facts that what is broken can be mended, who is lost can be found, that homes matter, that every life matters, that through God all things are possible, and that to live a love story in one's own life is a prerequisite to living a fully honest life.

*T*herefore, as surely as Our ancestors adopted Christianity, as surely as cavemen adopted the building of wooden huts and ancient savages eventually adopted holy matrimony and an appreciation for romance, We do, by authority of a common humanity eternal, solemnly declare Our interdependence with *T*he *U*nited *K*ingdom, *T*he *B*ritish *M*onarchy as well as *T*he *B*ritish

*C*ommonwealth and Western civilization that would not exist if not for a long series of adoptions. In additional support of this declaration of interdependence, *W*e pledge Our care, Our gratitude, and Our sacred honour.

National Expectations

National Expectations

Reader's Notes

National Expectations

National Expectations

www.ingramcontent.com/pod-product-compliance
Lightning Source LLC
Chambersburg PA
CBHW070138080526
44586CB00015B/1746